BUSINESS MANAGEMENT

IB DIPLOMA PROGRAMME

Loykie Lomine

OXFORD
UNIVERSITY PRESS

OXFORD
UNIVERSITY PRESS

Great Clarendon Street, Oxford, OX2 6DP, United Kingdom

Oxford University Press is a department of the University of Oxford. It furthers the University's objective of excellence in research, scholarship, and education by publishing worldwide. Oxford is a registered trade mark of Oxford University Press in the UK and in certain other countries

British Library Cataloguing in Publication Data
Data available

978-0-19-843760-4

10 9 8 7 6 5 4 3 2 1

MIX
Paper from
responsible sources
FSC® C007785
www.fsc.org

Paper used in the production of this book is a natural, recyclable product made from wood grown in sustainable forests. The manufacturing process conforms to the environmental regulations of the country of origin.

Printed in the UK by Bell and Bain Ltd. Glasgow

Acknowledgements

Photo credits:

Cover image: Southtownboy Studio/Shutterstock.
All other photos © Shutterstock.

Artwork by Q2A Media Services Pvt. Ltd.

The publisher would like to thank the International Baccalaureate for their kind permission to adapt questions from past examinations and content from the subject guide. The questions adapted for this book, and the corresponding past paper references, are summarized here:

Introduction (**Command terms**), **pvi**: **Define** N18 SLP1 TZ0 Q4(a), **Describe** M19 HLP1 TZ0 Q3(a), **Outline** M19 HLP1 TZ0 Q2(a), **State** M19 SLP1 TZ0 Q4(a); **pvii**: **Distinguish** N18 HLP1 TZ0 Q3(b), **Explain** M19 SLP1 TZ0 Q4(c); **pviii**: **Discuss** N18 SLP1 TZ0 Q4(d), **Examine** N18 HLP2 TZ0 Q8, **Recommend** M19 SLP1 TZ0 Q4(d); **pix**: **Calculate** M19 SLP1 TZ0 Q4(a), **Construct** N18 HLP2 TZ0 Q2(b)(i), **Draw** N18 SLP2 TZ0 Q3(c)(i), **Label** N18 SLP2 TZ0 Q3(c)(i), **Prepare** M17 SLP2 TZ0 Q2(b); Question practice, **p2**: M17 SLP1 TZ0 Q4(b); Question practice, **p3**: M17 HLP2 TZ0 Q3(b); Question practice, **p7**: M18 SLP1 TZ0 Q4(a); Question practice, **p7**: M18 HLP1 TZ0 Q3(b); Question practice, **p11**: N17 HLP1 TZ0 Q2(b); Question practice, **p11**: M17 SLP1 TZ0 Q3(b); Question practice, **p14**: M17 SLP1 TZ0 Q1(a); Question practice, **p18**: N17 HLP2 TZ0 Q3; Question practice, **p21**: M16 HLP1 TZ0 Q3(c); Assessment tip (Figure 1.7.5), **p25**: N17 HLP1 TZ0 Section C; Assessment tip, **p28**: M16 SLP2 TZ0 Q1(a); Assessment tip, **p28**: M16 HLP2 TZ0 Q1(a); Question practice, **p29**: N17 HLP1 TZ0 Q1(b); Question practice, **p35**: M17 HLP1 TZ0 Q2(b); Question practice, **p36**: M18 HLP1 TZ0 Q2(b); Question practice, **p41**: N16 SLP2 TZ0 Q5(b); Question practice, **p41**: M17 HLP2 TZ0 Q5(b); Question practice, **p42**: N17 HLP2 TZ0 Q5(d); Question practice, **p50**: M17 SLP1 TZ0 Q3(a); Assessment tip, **p53**: M16 SLP2 TZ0 Q2(a); Question practice, **p56**: N17 SLP2 TZ0 Q2; Question practice, **p61**: M17 SLP2 TZ0 Q1; Question practice, **p62**: M17 HLP2 TZ0 Q2; Question practice, **p65**: N18 SLP1 TZ0 Q4(b); Question practice, **p68**: M17 HLP2 TZ0 Q1(b)(i)(ii); Question practice, **p72**: M17 SLP2 TZ0 Q2; Question practice, **p75**: N16 HLP2 TZ0 Q1(b)(c); Question practice, **p81**: M18 HLP1 TZ0 Q4(b); Question practice, **p85**: N18 HLP1 TZ0 Q1(a); Question practice, **p86**: M17 HLP2 TZ0 Q4(a); Question practice, **p86**: N17 SLP2 TZ0 Q3(b); Question practice, **p88**: M18 HLP1 TZ0 Q4(a); Question practice, **p92**: M17 HLP2 TZ0 Q4(b); Question practice, **p93**: N17 SLP1 TZ0 Q4(b); Question practice, **p97**: M17 HLP1 TZ0 Q4(b); Question practice, **p98**: N18 SLP1 TZ0 Q2(b); Question practice, **p98**: M17 HLP2 TZ0 Q4(c); Question practice, **p99**: M17 SLP1 TZ0 Q1(b); Question practice, **p105**: N18 HLP1 TZ0 Q3(a); Question practice, **p110**: M18 SLP1 TZ0 Q3(a); Question practice, **p113**: M17 HLP1 TZ0 Q4(a); Question practice, **p114**: M18 SLP1 TZ0 Q2(b); Assessment tip, **p119**: M16 HLP2 TZ0 Q6; Assessment tip, **p119**: N17 HLP2 TZ0 Q6; Assessment tip, **p119**: N18 HLP2 TZ0 Q6; Table 6.1.1, **p122**: N18 SLP1 TZ0 Q4(d), M16 SLP2 TZ0 Q3(d), N17 HLP1 TZ0 Q4(d), N14 HLP2 TZ0 Q4(d); Question practice, **p123**: M17 SLP2 TZ0 Q3(c); Question practice, **p126**: N18 SLP1 TZ0 Q4(d); Examples, **p130**: N18 HLP2 TZ0 Q6, Q7, Q8; Examples, **p131**: M17 SLP2 TZ0 Q6, Q7, Q8; Question practice, **p134**: M17 SLP2 TZ0 Q7.

The author and publisher are grateful to those who have given permission to reproduce the following extracts and adaptations of copyright material:

Alzheimer's Association: 'Our Vision' statement from www.alz.org, reprinted by permission.

Although every effort has been made to trace and contact copyright holders before publication, this has not been possible in some cases. We apologise for any apparent infringement of copyright and if notified, the publisher will be pleased to rectify any errors or omissions at the earliest opportunity.

Links to third party websites are provided by Oxford in good faith and for information only. Oxford disclaims any responsibility for the materials contained in any third party website referenced in this work.

Contents

 Answers to questions and exam papers in this book can be found on your free support website. Access the support website here: www.oxfordsecondary.com/ib-prepared-support

This book provides coverage of the IB diploma syllabus in business management and offers support to students preparing for their examinations. The book will help you revise the study material, consolidate the essential terms and concepts, understand the assessment criteria and improve your approach to IB examinations. All topics are illustrated by annotated examples of student answers to previous exam questions, explaining why and how marks may be scored or missed.

DP business management assessment

All standard level (SL) and higher level (HL) students must complete the internal assessment and take papers 1 and 2 as part of their external assessment. Paper 1 is based on a pre-seen case study released by the IB three months before the exam. Paper 2 is based on unseen material. The internal and external assessment marks are combined, as shown in the following table, to give your overall DP business management grade, from 1 (lowest) to 7 (highest).

Assessment overview

Assessment	SL		HL	
	Task	Weight	Task	Weight
Internal	Written commentary	25%	Research report	25%
Paper 1	1 hour and 15 minutes exam	30%	2 hours and 15 minutes exam	35%
Paper 2	1 hour and 45 minutes exam	45%	2 hours and 15 minutes exam	40%

Overview of the book structure

The book is composed of several elements.

Five **units**, as in the IB DP business management syllabus:

- Unit 1: Business organization and environment

- Unit 2: Human resource management

- Unit 3: Finance and accounts

- Unit 4: Marketing

- Unit 5: Operations management

Each unit is divided into sub-units with summaries of the key syllabus content and useful content links.

Further sections:

- Evaluative questions worth 10 marks, as all the exam papers have *at least* one such question worth 10 marks. This section also explains in detail the markbands used by examiners.

- Extended responses, about the evaluative questions worth 20 marks; this chapter unpacks the five assessment criteria and provides tips to achieve high marks for the Section C extended responses.

- Internal assessment, explaining the task, the assessment criteria, with one example at SL and one template of structure at HL. This section also includes tips to avoid common mistakes.

- Practice exam paper 2: examples of IB-style practice questions like those found in paper 2, written exclusively for this book. These examples will give you the opportunity to test yourself before the actual exam, as they provide additional practice problems for the material featured in all the units. The answers and solutions are given online at: **www.oxfordsecondary.com/ib-prepared-support**.

Concepts

The following six concepts underpin the DP business management course:

- Change
- Culture
- Ethics
- Globalization
- Innovation
- Strategy

There is no universally accepted definition of these concepts; you are not expected to memorize the definitions that follow: what matters is your understanding of these concepts, both in general and in business management.

- **Change** refers to modification or transformation over time or across places. In business management, change is usually the result of internal or external influences. For example, externally, new competitors and new trends in consumer behaviour may lead an organization to adapt its objectives and operations; internally, the arrival of a new CEO may lead to a shift in the priorities of the organization's strategic plan.

- **Culture** refers to the norms, beliefs and values of a group of people. Sociologically, this could be within a country or a region – but organizations also have their own culture that develops over time. Within an organization, culture is shaped by factors such as the attitudes and backgrounds of internal stakeholders, as well as its history and other characteristics such as size and structure.

- **Ethics** refer to the moral principles and values that form the basis of how a person or an organization conducts their activities. In business management, it is important to realize that every decision may have moral implications, impacting on internal and external stakeholders and the natural environment. Ethics is present throughout the organization, from marketing communication to operations, from recruitment of new staff to accounting practices.

- **Globalization** refers to the increasing flow of ideas, financial transactions, goods and services around the world. A wide range of international forces (such as the increasing social, cultural, technological and economic integration) influence business organizations – and, in turn, business organizations shape these forces, contributing to the greater integration and understanding of countries and cultures. All businesses and consumers are influenced by global forces, directly or indirectly.

- **Innovation** refers to the addition of something new. In business management, this may be the incremental or radical improvement of a business idea, of a product or of a process, in order to be more successful or more competitive. For many business organizations, a key challenge is bringing in "the new" and managing the process of improvement in a sustainable way that does not create conflict.

- **Strategy** refers to the planned actions designed to achieve long-term goals. In business management, strategy is about the long-term planning decisions that organizations make in order to meet the needs and wants of their stakeholders. Strategy is about asking questions: what, why, when, how, where and who?

Command terms

In the exam questions, **command terms** are the words that tell you how to approach the question, especially in terms of depth. It is crucial that you understand these terms correctly. Before you answer a question, you should:

- Underline the command term.

- Look at the mark weighting of that question.

- Match your answer to the depth required for the command term.

In business management, examiners often say that many candidates do not achieve high marks because they do not pay sufficient attention to the command terms.

Command terms fall into four categories:

1. Some command terms assess your ability to demonstrate **knowledge and understanding** of the subject. These are the most accessible questions, worth 2 or 4 marks.

Command term	IB definition	Sample question	Note the following:
Define	Give the precise meaning of a word, phrase, concept or physical quantity.	Define the term *intangible asset*. [2 marks]	For such definition questions, you are not expected to refer to the case study or stimulus material. Note: *all* the terms in the five Units of the syllabus may be the subject of such a definition question, from "intrapreneur" (1.1) to "offshoring" (5.4).
Describe	Give a detailed account.	Describe two changes in the external environment that have affected *RDM*. [4 marks]	These two command terms are frequently used in business management exam questions. The questions may seem easy, yet many candidates do not achieve full marks because they sometimes write answers that are too *theoretical* or too *superficial*.
Outline	Give a brief account or summary.	With reference to *RDM*, outline one advantage and one disadvantage of Jan's leadership style. [4 marks]	In this context, *theoretical* means that the candidate does not take the case study into account, but writes a generic answer. *Superficial* means that the answer is too short; the text written by the candidate may not have nor add value: only copying an extract from the case study is not enough. Put another way, candidates often miss marks because they approach these questions as "reading comprehension" and only lift relevant passages from the text. These command terms are about knowledge and understanding of business management, not knowledge and understanding of the case study.
State	Give a specific name, value or other brief answer without explanation or calculation.	State two reasons for selecting a specific location for production. [2 marks]	Your answer may be very brief, just a few words or bullet points.

2. Some command terms assess your ability to demonstrate **application and analysis**. This is a more demanding task; these questions are usually worth more marks and your answers must be longer.

Command term	IB definition	Sample question	Note the following:
Analyse	Break down in order to bring out the essential elements or structure.	Analyse the impact of external opportunities and threats on the business strategy of company X.	Analysis requires a rigorous and systematic approach, as you have to pay attention to all aspects and their relationships with one another. The images of a chain (composed of several rings) or a tree (with roots, branches and leaves) can help you understand the idea of links and relationships.
Apply	Use an idea, equation, principle, theory or law in relation to a given problem or issue.	Apply the concept of diseconomies of scale to company X in 2020 compared to 2018.	Applying means making explicit links between "theory" and "practice": you show that you know the theory (for example, the terms or the models) and that you understand what they mean in the case of a specific business situation.
Comment	Give a judgment based on a given statement or result of a calculation.	Comment on the profitability, liquidity and efficiency ratios of company X.	
Demonstrate	Make clear by reasoning or evidence, illustrating with examples or practical application.	Demonstrate why company X has decided to offshore to country Y.	

Continued on next page

Distinguish	Make clear the differences between two or more concepts or items.	Distinguish between the leadership styles of Sam and Finn. [6 marks]	This command term is frequently used in business management exam questions. One common reason why many candidates do not achieve high marks is that they write about A, then about B, instead of writing about the differences between A and B.
Explain	Give a detailed account including reasons or causes.	Explain two types of financial rewards, other than salary, that *RDM* might offer its engineers and computer scientists. [4 marks]	This command term is frequently used in business management exam questions. One common reason why many candidates do not achieve high marks is that they only describe facts, they do not write about the reasons behind these facts. In the example here, they would only describe the types of financial rewards (such as fringe payments and perks) without explaining why these financial rewards are appropriate for the company's engineers.
Interpret	Use knowledge and understanding to recognize trends and draw conclusions from given information.	Interpret the differences in the liquidity ratios between 2020 and 2018.	This command term is often used after a question to do with calculations; you are then asked to write an answer where you show that you understand the meaning of the results. IB business management examiners use the system called "OFR" which stands for "Own Figure Rule"; this means that you will achieve marks if you properly interpret your results, even if the results themselves are not correct.
Suggest	Propose a solution, hypothesis or other possible answer.	Suggest a suitable method of appraisal for employee group X in company Z.	

3. Some command terms assess your ability to demonstrate **synthesis and evaluation**. These questions are worth 10 marks or 20 marks. Your answers must be much longer. There are two sections in this book about how to tackle these types of questions.

Command term	Definition	Sample question	Note the following:
Compare	Give an account of the similarities between two (or more) items or situations, referring to both (all) of them throughout.	Compare the leadership style of manager A with that of manager B.	Should you have an exam question with one of these three command terms, remember that: • If you are asked to "compare", you must write about the similarities (as opposed to "contrast" about the differences). • If you are asked to "contrast", you must write about the differences (as opposed to "compare" about the similarities).
Compare and contrast	Give an account of similarities and differences between two (or more) items or situations, referring to both (all) of them throughout.	Compare and contrast how the two managers use different planning tools to make changes to their strategies.	
Contrast	Give an account of the differences between two (or more) items or situations, referring to both (all) of them throughout.	Contrast the marketing objectives of for-profit organization X and non-profit organization Y.	

Continued on next page

Discuss	Offer a considered and balanced review that includes a range of arguments, factors or hypotheses. Opinions or conclusions should be presented clearly and supported by appropriate evidence.	Discuss whether Sam should accept the offer of a takeover. [10 marks]	This command term is frequently used in business management exam questions. There are two main reasons why many candidates do not achieve high marks: 1 Some candidates forget to reach a clear response at the end of their answer: in the example here, the conclusion should clearly say "yes, Sam should accept the offer" or "no, Sam should not accept the offer". 2 Some candidates start with their final answer (for example "yes, Sam should accept the offer") and then give many reasons to justify this decision. The answer, however, can only come at the very end, in the conclusion, after having reviewed all arguments and counter-arguments, all perspectives – and not at the start, as this leads to a one-sided response.
Evaluate	Make an appraisal by weighing up the strengths and limitations.	Evaluate company X's investment opportunities using net present value (NPV).	Like the command term "discuss", the command term "evaluate" requires you to give a balanced answer, covering both positives and negatives, strengths and limitations. This is what the examiners will do with your own exam papers: they will evaluate them, considering their strengths and limitations.
Examine	Consider an argument or concept in a way that uncovers the assumptions and interrelationships of the issue.	With reference to an organization of your choice, examine the impact of ethics and culture on human resource management. [20 marks]	This command term is used in Section C questions of paper 2 where you are expected to write long answers covering numerous aspects about concepts (two of them) and contents (in the example here: human resource management, the second unit of the course) in a specific context (your chosen organization).
Justify	Give valid reasons or evidence to support an answer or conclusion.	Justify the reasons why company X has decided to merge with company Y.	
Recommend	Present an advisable course of action with appropriate supporting evidence/reason in relation to a given situation, problem or issue.	Recommend whether *RDM* should choose Option 1 or Option 2. [10 marks]	This command term is frequently used in business management exam questions. The two main reasons why many candidates do not achieve high marks is the same as for questions with the command term "discuss": 1 Some candidates forget to reach a clear response at the end of their answer: in the example here, "*RDM* should chose Option x because there are more advantages than disadvantages". 2 Some candidates write partial answers: for example in the answer here, only about the advantages of Option 1 and the disadvantages of Option 2, which leads to a one-sided answer that lacks balance.
To what extent	Consider the merits or otherwise of an argument or concept. Opinions and conclusions should be presented clearly and supported with appropriate evidence and sound argument.	To what extent has outsourcing the production of X been unsuccessful for company Y?	Should you have an exam question that starts with "To what extent", it is important that you follow the advice given about comparable command terms such as "discuss" and "recommend": • Consider a range of perspectives and viewpoints. • Write a balanced answer. • Reach a precise, explicit conclusion.

4. Some other command terms assess your **skills**, especially to carry out financial calculations and to construct diagrams.

Command term	Definition	Sample question	Note the following:
Annotate	Add brief notes to a diagram or graph.	Copy and annotate the product life cycle.	
Calculate	Obtain a numerical answer showing the relevant stages in the working.	Using the information in Table 1, calculate for Location A the payback period (*show all your working*). [2 marks]	This command term is frequently used in business management questions about finance. Many candidates do not achieve full marks because they forget to include the unit or the percentage sign.
Complete	Add missing information/ data.	Copy and complete the profit and loss account provided.	
Construct	Display information in a diagrammatic or logical form.	Using information from Table 1, construct a fully labelled balance sheet for *Papel* for the end of October 2018. [5 marks]	This command term is frequently used in business management questions, for example about balance sheets, profit and loss accounts, cash flow forecasts or break-even charts. It is synonymous with "prepare": you may be asked to "construct" or to "prepare" a balance sheet, the task is the same.
Determine	Obtain the only possible answer.	Determine the break-even point for product X.	
Draw	Represent by means of a labelled, accurate diagram or graph, using a pencil. A ruler (straight edge) should be used for straight lines.	Draw and label a product life cycle for Strutz's No.5 jeans. [2 marks]	This command term is frequently used in business management questions, for example about product life cycle and break-even analysis.
Identify	Provide an answer from a number of possibilities.	Identify two reasons why the owner has chosen a particular method of investment appraisal.	
Label	Add labels to a diagram.	Draw and label a product life cycle for Strutz's No.5 jeans. [2 marks]	This command term tends to be used together with "draw" to remind you to add key terms to a diagram such as a product life cycle or a break-even chart.
Plot	Mark the position of points on a diagram.	Plot the position of Mbarek's company on the position map drawn in your answer to part b).	
Prepare	Put given data or information from a stimulus/source into a suitable format.	Using the information above, prepare a fully labelled cash flow forecast for *Anubis* from January to March 2018. [2 marks]	This command term is frequently used in business management questions, for example about balance sheets, profit and loss accounts, cash flow forecasts or break-even charts. It is synonymous with "construct": you may be asked to "construct" or to "prepare" a break-even chart, the task is the same.

Exam guidance and strategies

Manage your time effectively: every year, students lose marks through time mismanagement. A common tendency is to spend too long on the first questions (possibly because they seem easier and more accessible) at the expense of the others. Note that the IB allows five minutes of reading time before the start of each exam; you can use this time to decide which questions you will answer, as there is usually a choice (for example: 2 questions out of 3 in Section A of SL paper 1 and HL paper 1, or 1 question out of 3 in Section C of SL paper 2 and HL paper 2). For business management exams, you notionally have two minutes per mark, so you should spend at least 40 minutes on the 20 marks question of Section C.

Read the question carefully: pay close attention to the command terms, to the way the question is formulated and what you are asked to do. You must answer the question asked, not a question that may seem similar and that you have pre-prepared and memorized. This is particularly important for paper 1 where too many candidates do not answer the questions asked, but write out responses that they have already learned.

Use business management terminology: show the examiner that you know the language of the subject – throughout your paper, and not just when you answer "definition" questions. Write about stakeholders and business strategies, make references to the business functions, show that you can fluidly and accurately employ terms such as capital expenditure, non-financial motivation, marketing mix, diversification, outsourcing, production methods, economies of scale – this way, your papers will read like business management answers, not generic, common knowledge ones.

Do

- Read the instructions on the cover of your exam paper to remind you of the exam regulations, such as the time allowed and the number of questions you should answer in each section.
- Underline the command terms in the questions and focus on these as you work through each question.
- Write a brief plan for the extended answer (Section C) in order to give your answer a logical structure.

- Observe the mark weighting of the sub-parts of structured questions.
- Complete the correct number of questions.
- Make sure that all your answers are legible and correctly numbered.

Don't

- Fill your answer with irrelevant content just to make it look better. Examiners are impressed by quality, not quantity.
- Leave the examiner to draw conclusions if you cannot decide (for example at the end of a question with the command term "recommend").
- Bend the question to fit your rehearsed answer.
- Spend too long on your best question at the expense of others.

Key features of the book

Topic summaries focus on the main points of the sub-units. They give you basic definitions and cover all the key contents on which you may be examined.

Annotated student answers show you real answers written by previous IB candidates, which mark they achieved and why. Positive or negative feedback on student's response is given in the green and red pull-out boxes. These examiner's comments will help you understand how marks may be scored or missed.

 Content link

Link to your IA

Links to your IA (internal assessment) help you connect your IA and your exam revision, as your IA is a case study where the course contents are applied.

Link to other sub-units

Content links to other sub-units connect different sub-units that you could revise together, as they offer complementary perspectives on the same topic.

QUESTION PRACTICE

An **exam paper icon** indicates that the question has been taken from a past IB paper.

›› Assessment tip

Assessment tips give advice to help you optimize your exam techniques, warning against common errors and showing how to approach particular questions and command terms.

Concept link

Concept links connect the contents of the sub-unit to the concepts of change, culture, ethics, globalization, innovation and strategy.

Test yourself

Test yourself features contain questions relating to the main text, which invite students to consolidate their learning.

›› Revision tip

Revision tips give advice to help you structure your revision.

1 BUSINESS ORGANIZATION AND ENVIRONMENT

You should know:

✔ Introduction to business management

✔ Types of organizations

✔ Organizational objectives

✔ Stakeholders

✔ External environment

✔ Growth and evolution

✔ Organizational planning tools (HL only)

You should be able to:

✔ explain the role of businesses in combining resources to create goods and services

✔ explain the four key business functions: human resources, finance and accounts, marketing and operations

✔ distinguish between the four economic sectors of activity, and explain the nature of business activity in each

✔ examine the main issues around entrepreneurship:

   ✔ what does it mean to be an entrepreneur (and an "intrapreneur")?

   ✔ why is entrepreneurship (and intrapreneurship) so important in business activity?

   ✔ why an entrepreneur may decide to set up a new business.

   ✔ what are the common steps to set up a new business?

   ✔ what are the common problems when setting up a new business?

   ✔ what is this document called "business plan" that entrepreneurs usually prepare?

This sub-unit gives you an initial framework to understand what businesses do, how they operate and how they are organized. It emphasizes the importance of "entrepreneurs" who set up new commercial ventures and are essential to business activity.

Topic summary

All businesses, from small start-ups to huge multinational conglomerates, are based on the same principles:

• They combine **resources** (human, physical and financial) with **enterprise** (entrepreneurial skills to turn a business idea into a commercial reality): those are the *inputs*.

• They produce (tangible) **goods** and/or (intangible) **services** for their customers: those are the *outputs*.

- They are organized in **four key business functions** (human resources, finance and accounts, marketing, operations) that are interdependent.

- They operate in at least one of the **four economic sectors**: primary, secondary, tertiary, quaternary; some organizations operate in several sectors. Sectoral change is possible through vertical integration; together with horizontal integration, it enables businesses to grow.

An essential element of business management is **enterprise**; this term can refer to one organization (an enterprise = a business venture) or to a skillset (also called **entrepreneurship**). **Entrepreneurs** are people who demonstrate enterprise and initiative to set up a new business. This may be for a range of reasons, such as finding a gap in the market, independence (being self-employed, as opposed to working for someone else) or personal interest and passion. The term **intrapreneur** refers to individuals who are entrepreneurial within their workplace where they may develop new products.

The process of setting up a new business differs country to country, especially in terms of legislation, but certain features are usually present:

- There must be a basic business idea (which can be market-driven or service-driven).

- Planning is important; it may involve carrying out initial market research to ensure that the idea is commercially viable, i.e. that there is sufficient market demand.

- Establishing legal requirements: in most countries, all new business must be registered with the local authorities.

- In many cases, the entrepreneur may need to raise funds to set up the business (**start-up costs**) and to write a comprehensive document (called a **business plan**) to attract funds and to support the launch of the new organization.

- New enterprises may fail for a range of reasons, such as unreliable suppliers or underperforming workforce, inappropriate target market, cash flow management problems, inappropriate location.

> **>> Assessment tip**
>
> The four interdependent business functions (human resources, finance and accounts, marketing and operations) are present in all types of organization. For the paper 1 case study, identify them in advance; even if you do not have a question specifically about this, it can help you better understand the case study.

Test yourself

Can you represent visually each economic sector in the form of a drawing or with symbols? This is not an exam question, but this creative challenge can help you check that you understand and remember the differences between them.

QUESTION PRACTICE

This question is based on the May 2017 case study of *Utopia*, a holiday resort located on the island of Ratu, in the Pacific Islands.

With reference to *Utopia*, explain the differences between secondary sector activities and tertiary sector activities. [4]

SAMPLE STUDENT ANSWER

Secondary sector activities:

Secondary sector activities are determined as the production phase. This means that in the case of Utopia, the phase when the villas were being built. First by John and then by the local craftsmen. This had to be redone when the natural disaster in 2016 happened.

Tertiary sector activities:

Tertiary sector activities include the sale of the product to the customer. This means that, in this case the many different services, such as the boat drive and the villas are sold to the customer.

▼ The candidate shows that they know the meaning of "secondary sector" and "tertiary sector" however they did not answer the question asked: they answered "define secondary sector activities and tertiary sector activities" – they did not "explain the differences", as required by the command term of the question.

This response could have achieved 2/4 marks.

≫ Assessment tip

Command terms are very important – in business management, as in all other subjects. It is not enough to master the subject contents. You must follow the instructions of the command terms in order to achieve the highest marks, otherwise your answer will remain partial, even if you know the right answer. In the exam, before you start writing, make sure you closely read the question, unpacking its demands. Here, the candidate should have written about the differences between the two sectors, rather than defining one, then the other.

QUESTION PRACTICE

HS is a private limited company providing management consultancy services for public sector organizations like hospitals. *HS*'s consultants are all shareholders, and receive high salaries and profit-related pay. *HS* also gives its consultants freedom and encouragement to be intrapreneurs.

Explain **two** characteristics of an intrapreneur at *HS*.   [4]

SAMPLE STUDENT ANSWER

Response 1

An intrapreneur is an individual who is innovative, productive and constantly seeks to improve his or her activities and processes within the workplace and with his or her current job. One characteristic of an intrapreneur at HS is that he or she should be highly innovative, in the sense that they look for alternate methods or at how to make changes for more effective

▲ The candidate can define the term intrapreneur very well, especially the "within the business" element which is the key differentiator between entrepreneur and intrapreneur.

processes, products or ideas, yet within the business and focusing on their position and how they may contribute to the business. This then encourages self growth and development in the workplace environment.

▼ The overall answer remains too theoretical: there is no reference to the company *HS* and what it means to be an intrapreneur in that specific organization. For full marks, the answer should have been contextualized (i.e. written in the context of the organization).

Another characteristic of an intrapreneur at HS is that he or she should be able to use the available company resources and aim to achieve the company's goals and objectives without the use of external resources. They should not achieve creating new businesses, yet strive to achieve the goals in their organization through being resourceful. They should know how to improve through tampering with current business conditions, resources, and people.

This response could have achieved 2/4 marks.

Response 2

▲ Both characteristics are explained in the context of *HS* and the hospitals, i.e. with reference to the scenario presented. The answer is not only theoretical (showing the candidate's knowledge of what intrapreneurship means) but is also applied to the situation given.

Intrapreneurs are entrepreneurs within the organization that employs them; they are creative and innovative but not just for their own benefit. In the case of HS, their intrapreneurship is all about coming up with ideas and implementing them in the hospitals where they work, for the benefit of the hospitals and of the patients.

The HS intrapreneurs are consultants: it means that they do not risk their own capital (and this is different from an entrepreneur who starts up their business with all their savings). It means that HS intrapreneurs are safe as they do not take business risks themselves.

This response could have achieved 4/4 marks.

>> Assessment tip

Business management is an applied subject. You must always apply your answers to the scenario given (the long case study for paper 1, the short stimulus materials for paper 2). The only exception is definition questions such as "define the term".

>> Revision tip

The four business functions (human resources, finance and accounts, marketing and operations) are at the core of business management:
- They must be addressed in the business plan written by the entrepreneur.
- They help identify the areas of internal strengths and weaknesses of a SWOT analysis (see sub-unit 1.3).
- They correspond to the way the curriculum is structured (Unit 2: Human resource management, Unit 3: Finance and accounts, Unit 4: Marketing and Unit 5: Operations management).

Make sure you understand "the big picture" of how the course is structured, as it will help you structure your revision.

Content link

Link to your IA

As you work on your IA, find out how and when the organization was set up, by whom and why. Who was/were the entrepreneurs? What were their primary reasons and motivations? Did they write a business plan? Did they encounter particular difficulties? What were the first legal requirements? Even if you do not write about all this in your IA, these questions can help your IA research, and your IA gives you the chance to learn more about the contents of this sub-unit in context.

Content link

Link to other sub-units

- This sub-unit introduces unit 1 in general, so all other sub-units 1.2 to 1.7 are closely linked to it.

- Sub-unit 3.1 is closely linked as business plans must mention the intended sources of finance of the new business (for example loan capital, the most common one).

Concept link

The concepts of **culture** and **innovation** are closely linked to this sub-unit:

- Entrepreneurship is more encouraged in some **cultures** than others; in some countries, setting up a business and failing and trying again is not regarded negatively, whereas others are more risk-adverse.

- Entrepreneurship and intrapreneurship are closely linked to **innovation**: entrepreneurs and intrapreneurs want to try and do something new, or something different, from inventing and commercializing new products to redesigning ways of thinking and operating within an organization.

1.2 TYPES OF ORGANIZATIONS

You should be able to:

✔ distinguish between private and public sector

✔ discuss the main features of the following three types of for-profit (commercial) organizations:

    ✔ sole traders

    ✔ partnerships

    ✔ companies/corporations

✔ discuss the main features of the following three types of for-profit social enterprises:

    ✔ cooperatives

    ✔ microfinance providers

    ✔ public-private partnerships (PPP)

✔ discuss the main features of the following two types of non-profit social enterprises:

    ✔ non-governmental organizations (NGOs)

    ✔ charities.

This sub-unit classifies all organizations in a small number of categories, depending on whether they are established as "for-profit" or "non-profit". It also emphasizes that some organizations have a social mission: they are called "social enterprises".

Topic summary

The **public sector** refers to government-owned and government-operated organizations (for example public hospitals, the army or the police) whereas the **private sector** refers to organizations that are privately owned; they can be profit-making (for example a company) or non-profit making (for example a charitable organization).

The three main types of for-profit (commercial) enterprises (**sole traders, partnerships** and **companies/corporations**) have different legal status and are suitable for different types of businesses, according to factors such as size, ownership, liability and finance.

A **social enterprise** is a business which has a social purpose; it can be profit-making (for example a housing **cooperative** or a **microfinance provider**) or non-profit (for example a **charity** or an **NGO** which uses its **surplus** to advance the social cause it is defending).

Types of organizations, their legal status and even their names vary a lot from country to country, but there are standard features that you must know about, as well as their respective advantages and disadvantages (for example, a sole trader has total control over all important decisions, but with unlimited liability in case of faults, debts or mistakes).

>> **Revision tip**

A common misunderstanding noted by examiners is that many candidates wrongly believe that sole traders always work on their own. The word "sole" does not mean that they work alone: a sole trader may have employees.

>> **Revision tip**

Although the word "liability" is not mentioned in the curriculum (so you will not have an exam question specifically about it), it is important that you understand what it means, as it constitutes a key difference between a sole trader and a limited company. A sole trader is responsible (i.e. liable) for all the debts of the business: this is called "unlimited liability". A limited company is called "limited" because it has "limited liability": in case of a problem (e.g. bankruptcy) the investors (shareholders) can only lose up to the value of their shares, and nothing more. They are not responsible for the other debts the company may have. (In a balance sheet, the term "liabilities" refers to what the company owes to other firms, for example debts or payment to suppliers).

>> **Revision tip**

There are eight types of organization in total: sole traders, partnerships, companies/corporations, cooperatives, microfinance providers, public-private partnerships (PPP), non-governmental organizations (NGOs) and charities. You must be able to define each one, to explain its main features, also to compare and contrast it to other types, especially the three types of commercial organization. You also must be able to recommend the most appropriate one to a given situation; to do so, you must understand their respective advantages and disadvantages.

Define **two** characteristics of a charity. [2]

A charity's goal is for the betterment of the world rather than profit-oriented. Charities often operate more ethically than a typical business. Also, charities depend largely on donations rather than selling a good or service for cash inflow.

▲ This answer scored well as the two characteristics are correct: 1) the reference to a social cause (as opposed to being profit-making), 2) the reference to donations as a source of income.

This response could have achieved 2/2 marks.

▶▶ Assessment tip

You may have an exam question asking you to **justify** a particular type of organization or a change in its legal status, for example a sole trader who has decided to enter in a partnership with others, or to form a private limited company. The command term "justify" means to "give valid reasons or evidence to support an answer or conclusion". In this case, you would need to identify the reasons, explain them and evaluate them, with reference to their advantages and disadvantages in the context given. This is a demanding task.

Likewise, you may be asked to **recommend** a legal type to a given organization. The command term "recommend" means "present an advisable course of action with appropriate supporting evidence/reason in relation to a given situation, problem or issue" so you would need to identify the reason for your recommendation (for example, a partnership), explain these reasons and evaluate them, with reference to their advantages and disadvantages in the specific case. Your answer to such a question should therefore be quite long, as there is a lot to cover.

This question refers to an entrepreneur called Su who is setting up a social enterprise called *Afghan Sun* (AS), which is going to operate as a private limited company.

Explain the advantages for Su of forming *AS* as a private limited company. [6]

Response 1

A private limited is a company in which the shares are not offered for the public only for family members and friends. The shareholders of private limited companies enjoy limited liability.

▼ In this short answer, the candidate demonstrates some knowledge (about shares and limited liability) but this is not sufficiently developed: they should have explained what shares are (possibly with reference to dividends), what "limited liability" means, and why it is an advantage.

This response could have achieved 2/6 marks.

Response 2

Although AS is a social enterprise but Su has decided to operate as a private limited company. This could bring many advantages to her as an entrepreneur to her starting organization AS. One of the advantages is that:

- because it is a private limited company, therefore the shares can only be sold to friends or family, this way she can have a wider control over the shareholders and that she has limited liability meaning in case of bankruptcy she will only lose the amount that she had invested.

- Another advantage is that in comparison with the public-limited companies, a private-limited company is easier to start up because the shares shouldn't be on the stocks and therefore again decision makings are faster and easier too.

▼ The topic of selling shares (to friends and family) is only briefly mentioned; the candidate does not explain why it is an advantage. The reference to "wider control over the shareholders" is not sufficiently clear, although the candidate seems to understand what a private limited company is.

▲ Limited liability is explained as an advantage.

▼ The causal link between easier set up and shares not on the stocks is not entirely clear.

▲ The reference to decision-making is interesting; it is linked to the topic of control mentioned before.

Note: Overall the candidate understands key advantages that private limited companies have (for example in terms of selling shares and limited liability). However the answer is not sufficiently contextualized, i.e. applied to the case study.

This response could have achieved 4/6 marks.

Revision tip

A common misunderstanding is that many candidates wrongly believe that "business owner" is the same as "business manager". Owners and managers are the same in some cases, for example for sole traders and some partners, but usually managers are employed by the company, by the shareholders (who are the real owners); the business does not belong to the managers, they work for it and receive a salary, like the other employees.

Content link
Link to your IA

As you work on your IA, find out about the legal status of your organization: is it a sole trader, a private limited company, or maybe a public company? If it is a limited company, you could enquire about the number of shareholders and the dividends they receive. If it is a partnership, you could find out if the partners share the profits equally or not. Your IA gives you the chance to learn more about the contents of this sub-unit in context.

Content link
Link to other sub-units

- Sub-units 1.2 and 1.3 are linked because there is often a relationship between the broad aim of the organization and its legal status (for example a small, non-profit making organization that exists for the public good will be a social enterprise, such as a charity).

- Sub-units 1.2 and 2.2 are linked because there is often a relationship between the legal type of the organization and its structure (for example a small partnership will not be structured like a large public limited company).

Concept link

The concepts of **culture** and **change** are linked to the topic of types of organization:

- **Change**, because small organizations, as they grow and expand, often change status (for example a sole trader who decides to become a private limited company, with two key benefits: the ability to raise more capital through shares and the protection offered by the limited liability).

- **Culture**, because the culture that develops within an organization often reflects the type of organization (for example a small local charity relying on donations may not have the same values as a large multinational company or MNC).

1.3   BUSINESS OBJECTIVES

You should be able to:

✔ distinguish between vision statement and mission statement, aims, objectives, strategies and tactics

✔ discuss the relationships between aims, objectives, strategies and tactics

✔ discuss the need for organizations to change objectives and innovate in response to changes in internal and external environments

✔ discuss reasons why organizations set ethical objectives and the impact of implementing them

✔ discuss the evolving role and nature of corporate social responsibility (CSR)

✔ prepare the SWOT analysis of an organization, and use it to evaluate the organization

✔ apply the Ansoff matrix to an organization and use it to recommend appropriate strategies.

This sub-unit emphasizes the importance of long-term business objectives, including ethical objectives. It introduces two important models: SWOT analysis and Ansoff matrix.

Topic summary

Most organizations have a written **mission statement**, which describes what they do, or a **vision statement**, which is more forward-looking and aspirational, or both.

All businesses develop through setting and reaching **objectives**; these objectives can be **strategic** (long-term), **tactical** (short-term) or **operational** (day-to-day). Objectives are usually part of a wider organizational **aim**, which is linked to the organization's vision.

Why might businesses need to change objectives and strategies?

- Because of changes in the **internal** environment, for example a new chief executive officer (CEO) who has her own ideas for the direction of the organization, or because the organization itself is changing, either radically (for example through a merger with another company) or gradually (and previous strategies written many years ago are not suitable anymore).

- Because of changes in the **external** environment, for example new legislation regarding health and safety may mean that previous practices are not legal any longer, or customers may expect the organization to follow more ethical and sustainable principles.

Two main tools (models) are used to set business objectives:

- The **SWOT analysis** framework, where the four business functions (human resources, finance and accounts, marketing, and operations) help to identify the *internal* strengths and weaknesses of an organization (whereas a STEEPLE analysis helps to identify the opportunities and threats coming from the *external* environment):

	Positive	**Negative**
Internal (from business functions)	Strengths	Weaknesses
External (from STEEPLE)	Opportunities	Threats

▲ Figure 1.3.1 SWOT analysis

- The **Ansoff matrix**, which considers both product and market, each time in terms of "existing" and "new":

		Product	
		Existing	**New**
Market	**Existing**	Market penetration	Product development
	New	Market development	Diversification

▲ Figure 1.3.2 The Ansoff matrix

SWOT analysis and the Ansoff matrix are very important models that all candidates should know and understand; however examiners always note the same common errors:

- In the Ansoff matrix, some candidates often get confused between "product development" and "market development". When they draw the matrix, some candidates forget to label the rows and columns ("Existing product", "New product" etc.) so the model is not complete.

- In the SWOT analysis, many candidates forget that the Opportunities and Threats must be external (so for example they write that "workforce going on strike" is a threat or that "using social media for marketing" is an opportunity; this is not correct).

>> **Revision tip**

A common misunderstanding noted by examiners is that many candidates get confused between "mission statement" and "vision statement":

- The mission statement is a description in the present tense, for example the charity *Reach Out* (the subject of the Paper 1 case study in 2011) has been set up to support the families of children with autism. It has the following vision statement: *"no child with autism will be left behind"* and the following mission statement:

  Reach Out provides online support for families of children with autism and offers them communication resources at a greatly reduced price.

The vision statement is clearly about the future and is aspirational, whereas the mission statement describes what the organization does.

- The vision statement is a description of where the organization wants a *community*, or *the world*, to be as a result of their actions and services, for example the charity *Alzheimer's Association* (https://www.alz.org/about/strategic-plan) has the following vision statement:

  A world without Alzheimer's disease.

Make sure you understand how mission and vision statements differ, and also what is important about the messages they give to their stakeholders.

QUESTION PRACTICE

MSS is a school for girls located in Tanzania. It has a mission statement and a vision statement.

Explain, with reference to *MSS*, the purpose of the mission and vision statements. [6]

SAMPLE STUDENT ANSWER

Mission statement declares the underlying purpose of the business and states what the business is and what it does. Vision statement is basically the long-term goals and aspirations of the company.

▲ The answer starts well: the candidate shows that they understand the difference between vision statement and mission statement – and they apply the two to the case study.

It basically states what the business intends to achieve in the future. The main long-term goal of MSS is to achieve economies of scale by expanding their school to various cities and countries. This vision allows the staff and employees to realize what they are working towards. It also affects the turnover rate as employees who are not satisfied with the vision of the organization may leave the company. The mission statement allows the customer to understand the main purpose of the business. The mission statement affects the size of the customer base as the main purpose of the mission statement is to attract more students. The main purpose of MMS is to provide high quality education for girls from low income families.

▼ The wording is sometimes unclear, for example when the candidate writes "the main purpose of the mission statement is to attract more students". Yes, the school wants to attract more students, but this is not the purpose of their mission statement itself: the purpose of the mission statement is to communicate what needs to be done in order to achieve the vision.

▼ Towards the end of the answer, the candidate only copies extracts from the case study, for example about the purpose of the school ("to provide high quality education…"); this is not relevant, this is not the question.

Note: The beginning of the answer was better than the end, where the answer loses some clarity and focus.

This response could have achieved 4/6 marks.

QUESTION PRACTICE

John has two businesses on the island of Ratu in the Pacific Islands: a holiday resort called *Utopia*, composed of 24 villas, and a café called *JAC* where he sells fair trade coffee.

Explain the role of ethics in John's businesses. [6]

▲ Right from the start, the answer combines "theory" and "practice" i.e. the candidate shows their theoretical knowledge (of ethics in business) both in general and in the applied context of John and *Utopia*.

▲ The answer includes subject terminology all along (e.g. brand, brand image) which shows that the candidate masters all aspects of the subject well (with references to marketing, in this case).

▲ After explaining positive aspects of the role of ethics (especially about marketing), the candidate now writes about negative aspects (notably about finance).

Ethics play a role in both of John's businesses, but more so in Utopia. Ethics are actions taken based on morals and ideals. There are many ethical implications involved with Utopia. John's focus on the local community of the Pacific Islands provides employment opportunities and support for this population. His emphasis on buying ethically produced, fair trade materials (I.e. Aora Coffee) in favour of cheaper, but probably more unethical products is part of Utopia's brand. He has created a brand image of Utopia based on ethical practices and the local culture. In this way, the role of ethics for Utopia is not just part of John's personal beliefs, but is part of his marketing and Utopia's unique selling proposition. However, it can also be argued that Utopia has unethical elements, such as the fact that its presence is most likely negatively affecting the natural environment of its "beautiful location". Ethical practices are also more expensive (such as Aora coffee) and could be a contributor to Utopia's recent financial losses. JAC has less of an ethics-focused approach than Utopia, but is still based on fair trade Aora coffee rather than its cheaper and more unethical alternatives. Due to its educational activities and displays, customers can also be educated about the coffee's origins and fair trade background, which both spreads John's vision, and contributes to positive public opinion surrounding the JAC brand image.

Note: The answer is thorough and balanced. It could be even better, for example the candidate could have written more explicitly about corporate social responsibility (CSR), however this fulfils the criteria for a top mark.

This response could have achieved 6/6 marks.

 Content link

Link to other sub-units

- Sub-units 1.3 and 1.5 are linked because the STEEPLE framework will help you to identify the external Opportunities and Threats of your SWOT analysis.

- Sub-units 1.3 and 1.6 are linked because objectives must change as the organizations grow in size.

Content link

Link to your IA

As you work on your IA, find out about the strategic objectives of your chosen organization. Does it have a mission statement and a vision statement? Have they changed over time? Who is responsible for setting the strategic, tactical and operational objectives? Is business ethics an issue for your chosen organization? You have probably prepared a SWOT analysis of your organization – but how about the Ansoff matrix: can you apply it to your organization? Your IA gives you the chance to learn more about the contents of this sub-unit in context.

Concept link

The concepts of **ethics, change** and **strategy** are linked to the topic of organizational/business objectives:

- **Ethical objectives** are becoming more important for all businesses, in all organizational aspects (human resources, finance and accounts, marketing, and operations). An increasing number of businesses are becoming aware of their corporate social responsibility (CSR), and they set business objectives for several reasons, such as building up customer loyalty, creating a positive image and increasing profit.

- Organizational objectives must be regularly reviewed to respond to **changes** in the internal and external environments; some changes can be anticipated (for example customer trends or patterns in demographics affecting the workforce), others cannot (for example a financial crisis in the national economy or the arrival of a strong competitor in the market).

- Businesses often work with documents called "**strategic** plans" where they set their objectives for the next five years; these plans are usually reviewed halfway through, or even more often in fast-paced dynamic sectors and markets such as electronics, cyber security and fast fashion.

1.4   STAKEHOLDERS

You should be able to:

✔ identify the internal and external stakeholders of an organization

✔ explain the interests of internal and external stakeholders

✔ discuss possible areas of mutual benefit and conflict between stakeholders' interests.

This short sub-unit introduces a key term in business management: stakeholders. Stakeholders can be internal or external – but they are always affected by the actions of the organization.

Topic summary

The stakeholders are all the people who have an interest in the success of an organization because they are directly affected by its actions. One distinguishes between:

- **internal stakeholders**, such as employees, managers, shareholders
- **external stakeholders**, such as customers, suppliers, pressure groups or people in the local community.

A stakeholder may be an individual (for example the CEO of an organization) or a group (for example the government or local authorities).

Stakeholders have different **interests**; they may occasionally have very different opinions and come into **conflict** with one another. For example, the CEO of a factory may want to increase production to meet customer demand; this could lead to an increase in employment, but local environmentalists and the local authorities could be concerned by the subsequent pollution.

≫ Assessment tip

It can sometimes be ambiguous to decide if a stakeholder is internal or external, for example business consultants are usually external but when they are employed by a company, typically on a contractual basis, they become internal, so if you have an exam question specifically about internal or external stakeholders, it is better and safer to choose straightforward examples.

QUESTION PRACTICE

Utopia is a holiday resort located on the island of Ratu in the Pacific Ocean.

With reference to *Utopia*, describe the importance of **two** external stakeholders.   [4]

SAMPLE STUDENT ANSWER

Response 1

▼ This short definition is correct, however the question is not "define the term external stakeholder". This initial definition is not credited: this is not what the question asked.

> The article states that "John deliberately resists pressure from external stakeholders to expand Utopia's capacity". External stakeholders means individuals or organizations that are not part of the business but have interests towards business activities. Government and pressure groups can be external stakeholders as they saw the potential growth of Utopia. They think expanding its capacity can attract more tourists.

▲ The candidate correctly identified two external stakeholders: government and pressure groups, however they did not describe their importance. This is a partial answer.

This response could have achieved 2/4 marks.

≫ Assessment tip

For questions about stakeholders, you will always be asked to refer to a specific organization from the case study (paper 1) or the stimulus material (paper 2). Make sure that you consider this: do not write about trade unions in the case of a sole trader who works on their own and does not have any employees.

SAMPLE STUDENT ANSWER

Response 2

▲ The two stakeholders are identified: customers and suppliers – so at this point, the candidate has already scored 2 marks.

▲ The candidate tells us why customers are particularly important: not just as a direct source of income, but because the business relies on word of mouth promotion (a reference to the case study).

> External stakeholders refer to individuals or organizations who are not part of the business but have a direct interest in its operations. In this case, the two external stakeholders can be customers and suppliers. Customers are important not only because they buy the goods and services of the business but also because they promote the business; for example, Utopia relies heavily on word of mouth for promotion which is done by the

customers. Suppliers are important as they affect the price and quality of the product. For example, Utopia serves high quality coffee; however, it is expensive.

▲ The candidate tells us why suppliers are particularly important for the *Utopia* brand, with a financial dimension too (they supply ethically produced fair trade Aora coffee, however it is expensive (reference to the case study)). The answer is clear and thorough overall.

This response could have achieved 4/4 marks.

Link to extended responses (Section C)

In your extended responses (Sections C of SL paper 2, HL paper 1 and HL paper 2) you will need to refer to a range of stakeholders; this is assessed under "**Criterion E: Individuals and societies**". This criterion assesses the extent to which you can give balanced consideration to the perspectives of a range of relevant stakeholders, including individuals and groups, internal and external to the organization. As you prepare your revision materials and your case studies for Section C, make sure that you can write knowingly about several stakeholders, both internal and external. This diagram, which shows the comparative closeness of stakeholders to decision-making, may help you:

>> **Assessment tip**

If you are asked to write about two stakeholders of your choice, choose very different ones – for example for external stakeholders: customers and suppliers, like in the example above. If you choose two stakeholders who are too similar (for example the suppliers of locally grown organic food and the suppliers of fair trade coffee), the two parts of your answer could overlap too much and you might not achieve the maximum marks, as ultimately you only show partial knowledge.

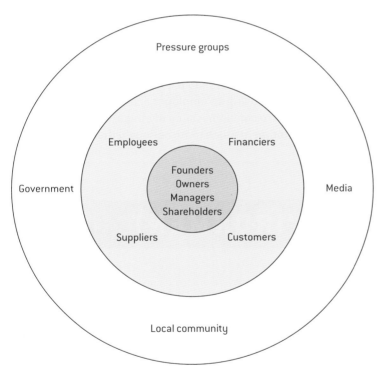

▲ Figure 1.4.1 The comparative closeness of stakeholders to decision-making

Looking at your section C case studies, can you readily write about *all* these stakeholders? And can you compare their level of interest in the success of the organization, and their ability to affect it?

 **Content link**

Link to your IA

As you work on your IA, identify the main internal and external stakeholders of your organization. Can you also identify some possible areas of conflict between some stakeholders? Your IA gives you the chance to learn more about the contents of this sub-unit in context.

Content link

Link to other sub-units

- Sub-units 1.4 and 1.6 are linked because a company's financial success and increase in profit will affect many stakeholders, both internally (such as shareholders who may receive more dividends) and externally (such as the government through more taxes).

- Sub-units 1.4 and 2.6 are linked because the conflicts between employers and employees, at the core of industrial relations, are conflicts between stakeholders who have different concerns and priorities.

- Sub-units 1.4 and 5.7 are linked because an essential aspect of crisis management is good, fast, transparent and honest communication with stakeholders.

Concept link

The concepts of **culture** and **ethics** are linked to the topic of stakeholders:

- **Culture**, because stakeholders may enter into conflict if they have different values and expectations. For example, the expatriate manager of the branch of a multinational company may need to adapt to the local culture if it is different from her country of origin, on aspects such as the culture of working long hours, or work-life balance, or dress code at work.

- **Ethics**, because some stakeholders may place ethics very high on their list of criteria when choosing an employer or a supplier. It is often said that millennials tend to consider issues of ethics, sustainability and impact on the environment much more seriously than previous generations.

1.5   THE EXTERNAL ENVIRONMENT

This short sub-unit introduces a key model in business management: STEEPLE – an acronym that considers the many external factors that may have an impact on an organization.

You should be able to:

✔ prepare and interpret the STEEPLE analysis of an organization

✔ discuss the consequences of changes in some external STEEPLE factors for an organization's objectives and strategic decisions.

Topic summary

STEEPLE is a simple framework that aims to list and classify, as comprehensively as possible, all **external** areas where changes may have an impact on an organization, considering: **s**ocial, **t**echnological, **e**conomic, **e**thical, **p**olitical, **l**egal and **e**cological factors.

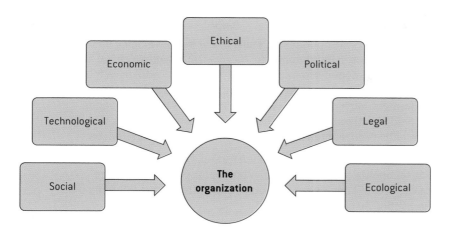

▲ Figure 1.5.1 STEEPLE analysis

The following table shows examples of common factors in a STEEPLE analysis:

▼ Table 1.5.1 Common factors in a STEEPLE analysis

Social factors	Changes in demographics, in lifestyle
	Social mobility
	Trends, fashion, tastes
	Education
Technological factors	New technologies, new discoveries and inventions
	ITC, e-commerce
	Research and Development (R&D)
Economic factors	Economic growth or recession
	Employment, unemployment, inflation, interest rates
	Exchange rates between currencies
Ethical factors	Changes of value in society
	Increase in CSR and fair trade practices, codes of business behaviour
	Corruption, anti-corruption
Political factors	Elections resulting in changes to government policies and priorities
	Political stability or instability
	Lobbying
Legal factors	Changes in legislation (that may affect employment, health and safety, production etc.)
	Competition laws between countries or blocs of countries
Ecological factors	Climate change, global warming
	Pollution
	Depletion of non-renewable resources

STEEPLE is a model that keeps developing. It used to be only STEP (or PEST); further alternatives may be encountered, such as STEEPLED with "D" for Demographics.

>> **Revision tip**

A good preparatory exercise for your paper 1 exam is to prepare a STEEPLE analysis of the case study.

In your paper 2 exam, you will not be asked to create, from scratch, a STEEPLE analysis, as this would require too many sources and documents, and too much time. You may however be given extracts from a STEEPLE analysis with questions about them, as in the example given in this sub-unit.

QUESTION PRACTICE

1 Pedro

Pedro is a farmer who operates as a sole trader in a developing country. Like other farmers in his community, he grows oranges, which are sold to buyers in developed communities and large cities. Working in the primary sector often results in very low income and poverty for some of the farmers. Most children do not go to school, as they are needed in the fields for manual work. Cooperation between the farmers in this community is very limited due to linguistic and cultural differences.

Recently, farmers' incomes have fallen further. Pedro has conducted social, technological, economic, environmental, political, legal and ethical (STEEPLE) analysis and identified two main external threats that are impacting on farmers' incomes:

- competition from orange producers from developed communities and large cities with improved technology and higher productivity rates

- a severe and sustained drought affecting the level of orange production in all developing countries.

Explain how each of the two external threats arising from the STEEPLE analysis would have impacted on farmers' incomes in the developing world.   [4]

Notes on the question: The two threats are explicitly stated in the second paragraph. The aim of this question is to assess your ability to interpret these two threats, about technological and ecological factors, explaining their impact on farmers' income.

The logical way to structure this question is to write two short paragraphs, each one about one of the threats. Some candidates tend to only copy the text given, or paraphrase it, rewriting it with slightly different words, yet with no "added value". The examiner wants to see your own text, your ability to express ideas in your own words, even if you think that the case study includes key elements of the answer and is very well written.

SAMPLE STUDENT ANSWER

The first threat is about the T for Technology. The orange producers in rich developed countries have access to a range of new technologies, for example chemical pesticides, crop selection and genetically modified seeds, resulting in higher productivity rates, i.e. more oranges per tree. With more oranges in the market, the price of oranges will decrease, (law of supply and demand) which means a decrease in revenue for Pedro and other farmers in developing countries.

▲ The impact is well explained, with reference to the given context.

The second threat is about the E for Environment. Because of drought, global warming and climate change, Pedro and the other farmers produce less oranges than before, so they have less oranges to sell.

▼ The impact is correct, but the explanation could be more developed for 2 marks.

This response could have achieved 3/4 marks.

Content link
Link to other sub-units

- Sub-units 1.5 and 1.3 are linked because your STEEPLE analysis will inform the external elements of your SWOT analysis (the Opportunities and the Threats).

- Sub-units 1.5 and 4.7 are linked because entering into international markets poses many challenges (for example legally because different countries have different laws about product standards, consumer protection, advertising and intellectual property rights).

- Sub-units 1.5 and 5.4 are linked because of the choice of location (or relocation) of a business (or one of its branches): some of the factors to consider can be identified by a STEEPLE analysis (for example about the labour pool or the availability of technological infrastructure).

Content link
Link to your IA

As you work on your IA, you should prepare a comprehensive STEEPLE analysis of your organization. Depending on your research question, it may not be directly relevant for your IA itself, but it will help you consolidate your learning from this sub-unit – and you will realise that many external factors may actually affect organizational decisions.

Concept link

The concepts of **culture, innovation** and **ethics** are linked to the topic of external environment:

- **Culture**, because the S of STEEPLE covers aspects that may be described as "socio-cultural" such as gender equality, lifestyle and living conditions.

- **Innovation**, because the T of STEEPLE, covering technological growth, automation and research, includes innovation (bearing in mind that innovation goes beyond technology).

- **Ethics**, because one of the Es of STEEPLE stands for ethics, so ethical factors must be considered (such as CSR, confidentiality, societal trust, corporate governance) as well as their possible absence (bribery, corruption).

1.6   GROWTH AND EVOLUTION

You should be able to:

✔ explain "economies of scale" and "diseconomies of scale"

✔ compare and contrast the advantages of being a small versus large organization

✔ distinguish between internal growth and external growth

✔ discuss the following methods of external growth:

    ✔ mergers and acquisitions (M&As) and takeovers

    ✔ joint ventures

    ✔ strategic alliances

    ✔ franchising

✔ discuss the role and impact of globalization on the growth and evolution of businesses

✔ discuss the reasons for the growth of multinational companies (MNCs) and their impact on host countries.

This sub-unit introduces important terms (such as "economies of scale") and processes (such as "external growth") which help understand why and how businesses may change and grow (e.g. through "joint ventures" or "franchises").

Topic summary

Economies of scale describes the reduction in average unit cost as a business increases in size. The opposite is **diseconomies of scale**: an increase in average unit cost as the business increases in size. Economies of scale are desirable; they may be due to internal factors (such as purchasing in bulk and getting discounts from suppliers) or external factors (such as concentration of customers in one area); likewise, diseconomies of scale may be due to internal factors (such as "over-specialized" managers) or external factors (such as a shortage of skilled workers meaning that the business may have to pay them higher wages to retain them).

Not all businesses want to expand. Large organizations have many advantages (including economies of scale, higher status and increased market share); however small organizations have many advantages too (such as greater focus on customers and competitive advantage in small niche markets).

Internal (organic) growth refers to the slow growth of a business occurring "from within", i.e. out of its existing operations; risks are limited, and expansion is often self-financed using retained profits. **External (fast-track) growth** is quicker but riskier; it involves some arrangements to work with another existing business. The four main methods of external growth are:

- **Mergers and acquisitions (M&As)**, when the businesses are completely integrated, thus becoming bigger (the term "**hostile takeover**" refers to an acquisition unwanted by the business acquired).

- **Joint venture,** the creation of a separate business entity by the two "parent" companies, for a finite period of time; the two companies still exist separately (so they can be described as "partners" in the joint venture).

- **Strategic alliances**, agreements by two (or more) companies to work together for mutual benefit; unlike a joint venture, no new business is created.

- **Franchising**, a process whereby an original business (the franchisor) sells to another business (the franchisee) the right to use its business model, brand and products. Franchises are very common in most countries, from McDonalds to The Body Shop. Franchises have many advantages for the franchisor (for example no risk, but financial gains) and for the franchisee (as for example the product already exists and is usually well-known); however there are many disadvantages too (for example the franchisee has no control over what to sell, and the franchisor could see its image suffer if the franchise fails).

In the context of globalization, **multinational companies (MNCs)** that operate in more than one country have grown rapidly, thanks to improved communications, fewer trade barriers and market deregulation. MNCs have both positive and negative impacts on the countries where they operate: positive impacts such as economic growth (through employment opportunities) and possibly infrastructure projects, but also negative impacts such as profits being sent back to headquarters abroad and loss of market share for local businesses.

>> **Revision tip**

Most terms in business management may be defined in several ways, using synonymous expressions; for example you could define **franchise** as a contract or an agreement or a relationship between two businesses or two organizations. A small number of terms, however, have a specific technical definition that you must memorize by heart, such as **economies of scale**, the reduction in average unit cost as a business increases in size.

QUESTION PRACTICE

TM is a chain of supermarkets which has historically used internal growth to develop, as its attempts at external growth through franchising were unsuccessful.

Explain the advantages for *TM* of internal growth rather than external growth. [6]

SAMPLE STUDENT ANSWER

Response 1

Internal growth means it comes from inside the company with their own money. They open more stores without borrowing money from external sources like banks as they have to repay with interest.

▼ The candidate seems to confuse "internal/external growth" and "internal/external source of finance". Little may be credited in this answer, except the idea that "internal" means "from inside the company".

This response could have achieved 1/6 marks.

Response 2

Internal growth means expansion from within the business, for example by product development, market development, or increasing the number of business units and their location.

The advantages of internal growth are: less risk than external growth, builds on the company's strength (for example its brand name), more control.

The disadvantages of internal growth are: slow growth, hard to build a market if not already a market leader, may miss opportunities to collaborate with other companies (synergies).

▼ The candidate has some secure and correct knowledge about the topic of internal growth. The answer however is only theoretical. The candidate seems to write only what they have memorized; the answer here reads like a summary from a textbook. The section of the answer about "disadvantages" is not relevant. There is no application to the business (*TM*). The candidate is not using relevant information from the case study (such as the unsuccessful franchising and the system of rigid control that may be difficult to implement with strategies of external growth).

This response could have achieved 3/6 marks.

Response 3

Internal growth has many advantages for TM:
Internal growth is easy for TM because of their brand name is famous: when they open a new supermarket, they will get customers because everybody knows them, like Walmart.

▲ This is a good answer. The points made are not always written as in a textbook, but this is not a problem at all: the candidate, in their own words, shows that they fully understand the advantages of internal growth for *TM*. For a higher mark, the last point could be clearer, about franchising, as franchising is external.

They can keep the same managers and ask them to open the new supermarkets (like a team of professional TM supermarket openers).

They don't have to worry about working with other businesses or creating alliances and having disagreements and culture clash.

Staff know they can get promotion at work or move from one supermarket to the other, if they want to work in a different town, or at a different post.

They can keep control of what they sell and how, with their own brand and their own methods, so franchising could really work for them, but it says that it didn't).

This response could have achieved 5/6 marks.

Content link
Link to your IA

Depending on the size and type of the organization you study, topics such as joint venture and franchising may not be relevant for you, but other aspects from this sub-unit are relevant to all organizations. For your IA organization, what would represent "economies of scale" and "diseconomies of scale"? Why? And how could your organization grow (a) internally, and (b) externally? With such questions, your IA gives you the chance to learn more about the contents of this sub-unit in context.

Content link
Link to other sub-units

- Sub-units 1.6 and 2.1 are linked because growth involves workforce planning, so the company will need an HR strategy (either to employ more employees, or to lay off some employees in the case of a merger where some posts may become redundant).

- Sub-units 1.6 and 3.1 are linked because growth needs to be funded (either internally, usually through retained profit, or externally, for example through share capital or loan capital).

- Sub-units 1.6 and 4.5 are linked because growth and evolution have an impact on the company's marketing mix (especially if the company's products are at different stages of their lifecycles, needing different pricing strategies, different marketing approaches and different channels of distribution).

- Sub-units 1.6 and 5.6 are linked because research and development are important factors that lead the growth and evaluation of a company.

Concept link

The concepts of **change** and **globalization** are closely linked to the topic of growth and evolution:

- **Change**, because growth and evaluation are processes of change, usually about an increase in size and scope (though some sole traders and small companies purposefully decide to remain small).

- **Globalization**, because it has a significant impact on the growth of businesses for several reasons: increased competition (which may be good for consumers), greater brand awareness (and the development of a "local" unique selling point/proposition, or USP), skills transfer (especially as global firms have to hire locally and thus need to train local workers) and new business opportunities (especially through joint ventures, franchises or strategic alliances).

1.7 ORGANIZATIONAL PLANNING TOOLS (HL ONLY)

You should be able to:

✔ prepare, construct, apply and interpret the following four planning tools:

  ✔ fishbone diagram

  ✔ decision tree

  ✔ force field analysis

  ✔ Gantt chart

✔ assess the value of these four planning tools to an organization.

This sub-unit introduces four tools that organizations use to make decisions and plan projects.

Topic summary

Fishbone diagram

A **fishbone diagram** (also called Ishikawa's model) allows an organization to look closely at the causes and roots of a specific problem (such as loss of market share, or increased number of customer complaints). There are several versions with names that conveniently start with the same letter in English, for example the four Ms of Manufacturing (Manpower, Methods, Materials, Machines) or the four Ss of Administration (Surroundings, Suppliers, Skills, Systems). This qualitative planning tool is simple and can effectively help brainstorming and discussions. However, designing a valid and reliable fishbone diagram is difficult for several reasons: you need to know the organization well in order to identify the genuine causes, and you need to be objective and honest in order to justify the assertions made.

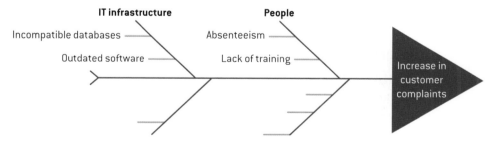

▲ Figure 1.7.1 Example of what a fishbone diagram looks like, with possible terms

Decision tree

A **decision tree** provides a visual structure to help managers make decisions by mathematically identifying the most suitable outcome, from a financial viewpoint. Outcomes are typically listed as "succeed" or "fail", with a probability percentage, or as optimistic, realistic and pessimistic. Calculations are then made to help identify the option with the best expected value (EV). This quantitative planning tool gives a clear answer to a complex decision, although it ignores qualitative factors that may be very important too.

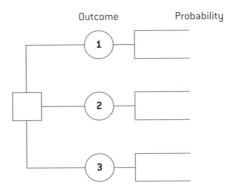

▲ **Figure 1.7.2** Example of what a decision tree looks like

Force field analysis

A **force field analysis** (also called Lewin's model, or just abbreviated as FFA) is used to compare the driving forces and restraining forces for and against a specific strategic question, and therefore to manage change by identifying in advance where there will be resistance to change (the restraining forces). This qualitative planning tool is flexible and can be applied to many situations; however, the relative weights given to the different forces may be very subjective and hard to justify.

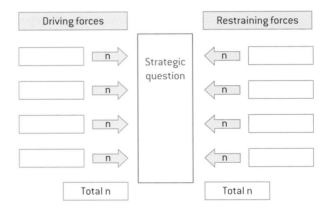

▲ **Figure 1.7.3** Example of what a force field analysis looks like

Gantt chart

A **Gantt chart** is used to plan a project comprised of several tasks (that may overlap), to create schedules (to manage time) and identify key deadlines (milestones). Gantt charts enable organizations to allocate resources appropriately, at the right time, and to keep an overview of the entire workflow. Presented as large tables, they give a clear picture of the progress and order of the various tasks, but they are based on estimates of the timings of each task and do not take into account important factors such as cost and quality.

	Task	Week 1	Week 2	Week 3	Week 4	Week 5	Week 6	Week 7	Week 8
1	Name of task 1	▓							
2	Name of task 2		▓	▓					
3	Name of task 3			▓					
4	Name of task 4				▓				
5	Name of task 5			▓	▓				
6	Name of task 6		▓		▓		▓		
7	Name of task 7								
8	Name of task 8								
9	Name of task 9								

▲ Figure 1.7.4 Example of what a Gantt chart looks like

>> **Assessment tip**

In your exam, you cannot be asked to create a fishbone diagram, a decision tree, a force field analysis or a Gantt chart from scratch: this would take too much time, requiring many resources and documents (for example to substantiate the relative weights given to each force in a force field analysis). You may however be *given* one diagram, and you may be asked to complete it (for example: carrying the final EV calculations of a decision tree) and to interpret the findings: the aim is to show that you can "read" and understand the document and how it can help decision-making in business management.

In November 2017, HL paper 1 candidates were given the following decision tree, in Section C:

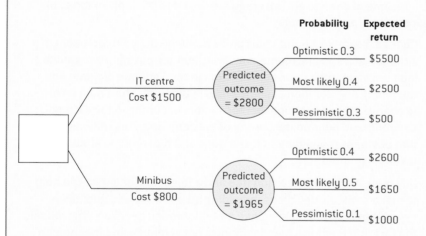

▲ Figure 1.7.5 Decision tree for IT centre and minibus

They were asked:

"Using the information (….) in Figure 1(.7.5), recommend either Option 1 (IT centre) or Option 2 (Minibus) (…)"

Put another way, candidates were expected to show their ability to interpret the decision tree, for example noting that setting up the IT centre costs much more than the minibus ($1500 vs $800, so almost double), however the predicted outcome is higher: $1300 for the IT centre ($2800–$1500) compared to $1165 for the minibus ($1965–800).

Revision tip

You must be able to identify the main advantages and disadvantages of all four planning tools. Considering factors such as objective/subjective and qualitative/quantitative may help you structure your evaluation.

 Content link

Link to your IA

HL students often use a Gantt chart to help plan their research, and they include it as part of their research proposal at the start of their IA. Is this what you did? How did this help you plan your work? Did this also help you to identify the limitations of a Gantt chart? How about the other three planning tools (fishbone diagram, decision tree and force field analysis) – did you use them for your IA? Or can they be used by your chosen organization to help make decisions or help plan projects? Again, your IA gives you the chance to learn more about the contents of this sub-unit by applying the tools introduced here.

 Content link

Link to other sub-units

- Sub-units 1.7 and 1.3 are linked because a force field analysis and a decision tree can help set a strategy and organizational objectives.

- Sub-units 1.7 and 4.2 are linked because a fishbone diagram can help to understand the marketing problems that an organization is encountering.

- Sub-units 1.7 and 5.5 are linked because a Gantt chart can be used for production planning.

Concept link

The concepts of **change** and **strategy** are linked to the topic of types of organizational planning tools:

- **Change**, because a Gantt chart and a fishbone diagram represent a situation at a specific moment in time: later on, possibly two weeks later or two months later, some factors in the fishbone diagram and the timing and duration of some tasks in the Gantt chart may have to change, because of unexpected factors occurring in the external environment, beyond the control of the company. This reflects the fact that business management is dynamic and that nothing should be taken for granted.

- **Strategy**, because a decision tree and a force field analysis can help to make strategic decisions, providing quantitative and qualitative reasons to help managers make a well-informed decision. This reflects the fact that business management is not scientific and that human factors must always be taken into consideration.

2 HUMAN RESOURCE MANAGEMENT

You should know:

- ✔ Functions and evolution of human resource management
- ✔ Organizational structure
- ✔ Leadership and management
- ✔ Motivation
- ✔ Organizational (corporate) culture (HL only)
- ✔ Industrial/employee relations (HL only)

2.1 FUNCTIONS AND EVOLUTION OF HUMAN RESOURCE MANAGEMENT

You should be able to:

- ✔ define human resource (HR) management, HR planning and HR plan
- ✔ explain the meaning and importance of labour turnover
- ✔ evaluate the internal and external factors that influence HR planning
- ✔ explain the common steps in the process of recruitment
- ✔ distinguish between different types of training
- ✔ distinguish between different types of appraisal
- ✔ define termination, dismissal and redundancy
- ✔ explain how changes in work patterns, practices and preferences affect both employers and employees
- ✔ discuss outsourcing, offshoring and reshoring as HR strategies
- ✔ discuss how innovation, ethical considerations and cultural differences may influence HR practices and strategies in an organization.

This sub-unit introduces the topic of human resources, one of the four essential business functions. It emphasizes the contents of the "HR plan" that all organizations should have in place and it outlines important HR strategies such as outsourcing and offshoring.

Topic summary

HR (human resource) planning, also called "**workforce planning**", is the continuous process of making sure that employees are selected, used and developed effectively, and estimating future HR needs. Numerous factors influence HR planning:

- External factors such as demographic change, change in labour mobility and new communication technologies.
- Internal factors such as changes in business organization (for example: restructure, streamlining) or changes in business strategy (for example: internal or external growth).

Labour turnover refers to the movement of employees into and out of an organization, over a given time period, usually a year; it is an indicator of how stable a business is. It is usually measured by the following formula:

$$\text{Labour turnover} = \frac{\text{Number of staff leaving over a year}}{\text{Average number of staff employed in a year}} \times 100$$

▲ Figure 2.1.1 Labour turnover

Although some labour turnover may be good for a business, a high labour turnover rate suggests that the business has labour problems, such as employees' dissatisfaction. The HR plan should make sure that the labour turnover rate is at an acceptable level.

The HR plan has four aspects:

1. **Recruitment**, in order to recruit the right person for the right job, which involves three parts:

   - Job identification (including writing the job description and the person specification – and deciding whether to recruit internally or externally).

   - The application process (job advert, with the use, or not, of an external agency).

   - The selection process (shortlisting, testing, interviewing).

2. **Training**, in order to ensure that employees receive appropriate professional development. There are different types of training: **induction**, **on the job** (through mentoring or shadowing), **off the job** (external training), **cognitive** (focusing on thinking and processing skills) and **behavioural** (focusing on emotional intelligence or stress management).

3. **Appraisal**, in order to evaluate employee performance. There are several methods of appraisal: **formative**, **summative**, **360-degree** and **self-appraisal**.

4. **Termination**, **dismissal** or **redundancy**, when an employee leaves, voluntarily or not.

Employers and employees are all affected by changes in work patterns, practices and preferences, such as teleworking, flexitime, job sharing and migration for work. Some organizations have developed new HR strategies such as **outsourcing** (**subcontracting**), **offshoring** (moving a business process to another country, often manufacturing or telephone support services) and even sometimes **reshoring** (back to the home country). Innovation, ethical considerations and cultural differences may also influence HR practices and strategies in an organization.

>> **Assessment tip**

Make sure you know the difference between terms such as "on the job" training and "off the job" training, or between "formative appraisal" and "summative appraisal", or between "termination" and "dismissal". You may be asked to define them: for this sub-unit, definition questions are quite common, especially in paper 2, for example:

Define the term *outsourcing*.   [2]

Or,

Define the term *offshoring*.   [2]

>> **Assessment tip**

In their answers about HR, some candidates use common words such as "firing" or "sacking". This is not appropriate and will not lead to top marks. When you write about HR, remember to use the correct technical terms, such as "made redundant", "laid off" or "dismissed".

>> **Assessment tip**

Candidates typically find the following difficult:

The difference between **redundancy** and **dismissal**.

The difference between **outsourcing** and **offshoring**.

Test yourself

Explain one example of offshoring that involves outsourcing.

Explain one example of offshoring that does not involve outsourcing.

QUESTION PRACTICE

The following question refers to the November 2017 case study, a school called *MSS* located in central Tanzania, in a rural remote area. In terms of human resources, a key problem for the school is the fact that teachers never stay very long: there is a high labour turnover.

Explain how the school could overcome high labour turnover.   [6]

SAMPLE STUDENT ANSWER

Response 1

Labour turnover is the movement of employees in and outside the business, a high labour turnover indicates negativity within the workplace of MSS due to language barriers and the remote area of the school, high labour turnover could be overcome by training teachers in the English language to diminish difficulties in teaching the students, another improvement can be made, it is the modification of the living accommodations provided to the teachers. It was of poor quality as reflected by one of the leaving teachers (line 44–45).

▲ The answer starts well: the candidate shows that they know the meaning of "labour turnover" and the fact that a high turnover rate is not a good sign for the organization.

▼ In the second part of the answer, the candidate only copies extracts from the case study. The passages are relevant, but the business management exam is not an exam of reading comprehension; for a higher mark, the examiner will reward subject knowledge about human resources, which is missing here.

This response could have achieved 3/6 marks.

Response 2

Firstly, the school should work towards motivating staff to continue working with the school. Using Herzberg's two factor theory, the staff are demotivated to work as the living conditions for the teachers are of poor quality. Furthermore, MSS pays teachers according to standard government pay scales, which may demotivate them from working harder. As such MSS should work towards correcting these hygiene factors and invest more in making sure the staff do not become demotivated to work and thus leave the school.

▲ The candidate shows knowledge from the course, with this reference to Herzberg's motivation theory well applied.

▲ The ideas flow logically and coherently (e.g. "As such…").

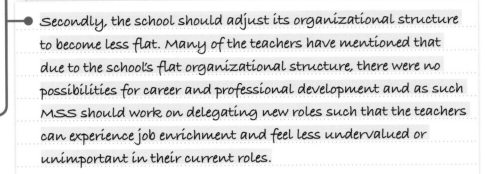

▲ The answer is well structured and easy to follow (e.g. "Firstly", "Secondly", "Thirdly").
The candidate uses relevant terminology throughout (with terms such as "organizational structure", "delegating", "job enrichment").

Secondly, the school should adjust its organizational structure to become less flat. Many of the teachers have mentioned that due to the school's flat organizational structure, there were no possibilities for career and professional development and as such MSS should work on delegating new roles such that the teachers can experience job enrichment and feel less undervalued or unimportant in their current roles.

▲ Several methods are explained in context; the candidate shows that they understand the case study, the story itself, but more importantly this answer is underpinned by subject knowledge: the candidate clearly knows about human resources, which is what the examiner is assessing here. For an even higher mark, it would have been good to see explicit references to the high staff turnover.

Thirdly, MSS should allow teachers more autonomy in their work in order to motivate them to remain with the school. As MSS requires the teachers to teach in English, some teachers found it difficult to do so and as such were less motivated to teach the students if they could not use their native language of Ki-Swahili, which is spoken by more of the students. Thus MSS should allow teachers to have more freedom in their lesson planning in order to motivate them to stay with the school.

This response could have achieved 5/6 marks.

Content link

Link to other sub-units

- This sub-unit introduces unit 2 in general, so all other HR sub-units 2.2 to 2.6 are closely linked to it.

- Sub-unit 5.2, about operations management, explores issues of location, outsourcing and reshoring, which are also addressed in this sub-unit, so you should revise them together.

Concept link

All six concepts are linked to the topic of workforce planning and HR management:

- Organizations that plan to grow must consider the impact in terms of human resources, as they are likely to need more staff: they will need an HR **strategy**.

- **Change** is a key factor in HR management: changes in the organization's staffing needs (for example, an increase in employment opportunities, or a decrease in the case of downsizing or outsourcing), as well as changes in society's expectations (for example millennials may prefer more flexible working patterns that differ from previous generations).

- Recruiters must be **ethical** and objective when selecting, interviewing and appointing new employees; discriminating against certain applicants is not only unethical, but it is also illegal in some countries.

- **Globalization** is both a cause and a consequence of offshoring: some companies decide to offshore in order to operate internationally, and this in turn tighten the links between the countries.

- For **cultural**, historical and political reasons, different countries have different legal systems regarding working hours. For example, in France since 2000, 35 hours is the legal standard limit and MNCs (multinational companies) operating in France must then adapt to this.

- **Innovation** often has HR implications: in the manufacturing sector, robotization and automation lead to a decrease in the need for lower-skill factory workers, but to an increase in the demand for higher-skill engineers.

Content link

Link to your IA

Even if your IA is not specifically about human resources, you can apply the contents of this sub-unit to your chosen organization. Do they have an HR strategy? Do they encounter particular issues to recruit or train staff? What is the staff turnover rate? What appraisal methods are in place? Do changes in work patterns, practices and preferences affect the organization? How about innovation, ethical considerations and cultural differences: do they affect it too? Your IA gives you the chance to learn more about the contents of this sub-unit in context.

2.2   ORGANIZATIONAL STRUCTURE

You should be able to:

✔ construct and interpret different types of organizational charts

✔ define key terms about organizational structure

✔ explain changes in organizational structures

✔ discuss how cultural differences and innovation in communication technologies may impact on communication in an organization.

This sub-unit focuses on the way organizations are structured, showing the relationships between the employees in different parts of the hierarchy.

Topic summary

An **organizational chart** is a diagram that shows the HR structure of an organization, outlining the formal roles, responsibilities and reporting lines.

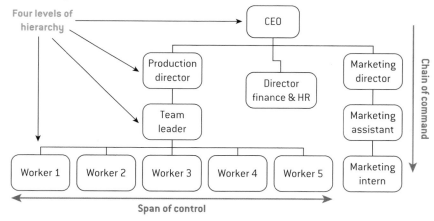

▲ Figure 2.2.1 Example of an organizational chart

▼ Table 2.2.1 Key terms to help describe the structure of an organization

Levels of hierarchy	The number of levels of responsibility and seniority in an organization, from the most "senior" to the most "junior".
Chain of command	The formal route through which decisions travel downward.
Span of control	Number of employees reporting to a specific line manager.
Delegation	When a manager gives authority for a particular decision to someone else, yet still holds responsibility for the outcome.
Centralization	Decisions are made by a small group in a senior position.
Decentralization	Decisions are made by managers throughout the organization (though senior managers retain control of key strategic decisions).
Bureaucracy	Rules and procedures within an organization.
De-layering	Removing layers of (middle) managers, reducing the levels of hierarchy.

Organizational structures can be flat (horizontal) or tall (vertical):

- **Taller organizational structures** are characterized by many levels of hierarchy, narrow spans of control, centralized decision-making, longer chains of command and limited delegation.

- **Flatter organizational structures** are characterized by fewer levels of hierarchy, wider spans of control, decentralized decision-making, shorter chains of command and increased delegation.

Departments are often organized by function (such as "Marketing" and "Finance"), though in some MNCs it may be more suitable to organize by region (by market) or by product (or families of product).

Other types of organizational structures include:

- **project-based organizations** (typically with a matrix structure)

- **"shamrock" organizations** with three types of employees: (1) core, (2) temporary, (3) contractual.

Changes in organizational structure may be due to internal or external factors, for example the need to hire more staff, including more managers, or the need to reconsider the entire structure after a merger.

Good communication (between employees, between levels of hierarchy and between departments) is essential in all organizations; innovation in communication technologies has helped communication, but cultural differences must also be taken into account.

≫ Assessment tip

Make sure you pay close attention to the **command term** at the start of each question. The expectations about the approach, contents and even length of your answer are different – and examiners pay very close attention to this. The following table gives you examples on the topic of change from a tall to a flatter structure.

Command term	IB definition	Example of question	Example of good answer
State	*"Give a specific name, value or other brief answer without explanation or calculation."*	**State** one advantage of changing the organization of company X from a tall to a flatter structure. [1 mark]	Fewer levels of hierarchy in company X.

Describe	"Give a detailed account."	**Describe** one advantage of changing the organization of company X from a tall to a flatter structure. [2 marks]	If company X adopts a flatter structure, there will be fewer levels of hierarchy from the top of the organization to the bottom: the pyramidal structure of the organizational chart will include fewer levels.
Explain	"Give a detailed account including reasons or causes."	**Explain** one advantage of changing the organization of company X from a tall to a flatter structure. [2 marks]	Adopting a flatter structure would have the following advantage: fewer levels of hierarchy make it easier and faster for communication to flow down the chain of command. This has been a source of problems in the past, with some middle managers complaining about this, so it would be beneficial for company X, for communication within the company and for middle managers' job satisfaction.
Analyse	"Break down in order to bring out the essential elements or structure."	**Analyse** one advantage of changing the organization of company X from a tall to a flatter structure. [3 marks]	Adopting a flatter structure means that company X would have fewer levels of hierarchy, which means a shorter chain of command and decentralized decision-making. As a result, many middle managers will be happy with this advantage, as they have complained about problems of communication at work; this is why the new CEO (chief executive officer) says that with a flatter structure and fewer levels of hierarchy, the atmosphere and work conditions will be better.

Concept link

All six concepts are linked to the topic of organizational structure:

- The structure of an organization usually reflects its **culture**, its history and its values. For example, a new high-tech start-up with six semi-autonomous employees working in an open office has a different culture from a well-established firm of lawyers, and this is reflected in the structure of the organization.

- The structure of all organizations **changes** over time; even today's largest MNCs started with a small number of employees. These changes can be gradual, with the slow addition of more employees and more levels of hierarchy, or more sudden, when for example two companies merge, which can result in a major restructuring.

- **Globalization** influences the structure of organizations that decide to operate internationally, as they may need to open branches and offices in different locations, which implies a change of structure.

- In 1962, the business historian Chandler published a book entitled *Strategy and Structure* which is now a classic text of business theory; in his book, he studied how successful American companies have always adapted their structures when they adopted a new **strategy**.

- How about **ethics** and **innovation**? How can you link these two concepts to the topic of organizational structure?

Content link
Link to other sub-units

- Sub-unit 2.3 about leadership and management is closely linked to this sub-unit about organizational structure because a manager's span of control and position in the organizational hierarchy will influence their approach, style, decisions and actions.

- Sub-unit 2.5 (HL only) about organizational culture is closely linked to this sub-unit too because the structure and the culture of an organization mutually influence each other.

Content link
Link to your IA

Even if your IA is not specifically about human resources, you can apply the contents of this sub-unit to your chosen organization. Do they have an organizational chart? (If not, you can draw one.) Is their structure tall or flat? How many levels of hierarchy are there? Has there been any change to the structure recently? Your IA gives you the chance to learn more about the contents of this sub-unit in context.

2.3   LEADERSHIP AND MANAGEMENT

This sub-unit focuses on the differences between management and leadership, including the range of leadership styles and what factors may influence them.

You should be able to:

✔ explain the key functions of management

✔ distinguish between management and leadership

✔ discuss the following five leadership styles: autocratic, paternalistic, democratic, laissez-faire and situational

✔ discuss how ethical considerations and cultural differences may influence leadership and management in an organization.

Topic summary

Management and leadership are closely linked. Managers can be leaders, and vice versa, but the two are different. One usually distinguishes between "**leader**" and "**manager**".

- The idea of "manager" and "management" is more about planning and organizing, setting and achieving goals by controlling situations.

- The idea of "leader" and "leadership" is more about inspiring and motivating staff, and about having a strategic vision for the organization.

There are numerous leadership styles, including the following five:

- **Autocratic** style, which emphasizes authority and control.

- **Paternalistic**, which places authority in a caring, family-like context.

- **Democratic**, which involves employees in the decision-making process.

- **Laissez-faire**, which gives employees more freedom and scope.

- **Situational**, which stresses the need to adapt to the situation, the decision and the context.

These five styles are not exclusive: they may overlap, for example a paternalistic leader often displays features of the autocratic leadership style. They all have advantages and disadvantages; they are all more appropriate in some situations than others.

Leadership styles and management styles are influenced by many factors, such as the personality of the leader/manager, their values, the workers, their motivation, the work environment, as well as aspects of **ethics** and **culture**. Ethical and cultural considerations shape the decisions made by leaders and managers, who in turn must take ethics and culture into account. This is particularly important in the case of ethical dilemmas (for example about distributing and selling clothes produced in "sweatshops") and of cultural differences (for example a branch manager who has just arrived in a new country may need to adapt her leadership style to the expectations, customs and values of her staff, otherwise they could enter into conflict with one another).

>> Assessment tip

Candidates usually understand management and leadership styles quite well, but their answers are sometimes too theoretical, i.e. not sufficiently applied to the case study (paper 1) or to the stimulus materials (paper 2). Remember, our subject is applied: the examiner wants to assess your ability to apply "theory" (your knowledge of leadership styles, with the proper terminology and the correct ideas) to "practice" (the examples themselves). If your answer is too theoretical, you will not be able to score top marks.

Further common mistakes in candidates' answers are comments that "autocratic leadership is bad" and "democratic leadership is good". The analysis and evaluation should be related to the situation and its variables.

QUESTION PRACTICE

This question refers to the May 2017 case study of John Ariki, an entrepreneur who has recently founded two businesses: a resort called *Utopia* and a café called *JAC*. John manages them both.

With reference to John, explain the key functions of management.   [6]

SAMPLE STUDENT ANSWER

Response 1

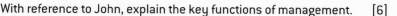

Managers are people who are higher in the hierarchy rank after the M.D. or owners. Managers are expected to:

be good planners

be good decision makers

be good organizers

control the business subordinates

to supervise

to run and motivate their subordinates.

▲ The answer starts well: the candidate shows some theoretical knowledge of the key functions of management, with the right terminology: decision-making, planning, control, supervision, motivating workers.

▼ The answer is not applied to the organization, nor to John (even though the question started with the words "With reference to John"). The answer is short and solely theoretical; moreover, the examiner cannot be sure that the candidate really knows what "decision-making" and "motivation" mean.

This response could have achieved 2/6 marks.

Response 2

One key function of management is organizing resources and maintaining production of high-quality products or services. John, as a manager of Utopia, has been organizing natural ingredients for meals from neighbouring islands and coffee from Aora. Also, by doing so, John has been able to provide both high quality and fresh food and coffee to its customers.

▲ Right from the first paragraph, the candidate applies their answer to John, explaining what the first abstract idea ("organizing resources and maintaining production") means in the context of John's restaurant.

▲ In the second paragraph, the candidate again refers to both "theory" and "practice", using correct subject terminology (about setting objectives and paternalistic leadership style). For an even higher mark, the examiner would expect a more developed answer, for example also mentioning control or coordination.

Another key function of management is setting objectives and motivating employees to reach this objective. John has set clear visions for both JAC and Utopia and setting clear objectives or visions no only gives direction to employees but also motivates them to work towards these visions. Also by adopting a paternalistic leadership style, John is able to discuss important decisions with his employees which will eventually give his employees motivation.

This response could have achieved 5/6 marks.

>> Revision tip

The name of our DP subject is "Business management" so you may need to show that you know what you are studying, what our DP subject is all about. All aspects of the syllabus, from marketing to finance, from HR to operations, ultimately aim at developing your understanding of how business organizations are managed. These principles apply to profit-making ventures ("businesses" strictly speaking) but also to non-commercial organizations, in the voluntary or public sector. In all these contexts, management is about planning, organizing, allocating resources, coordinating and controlling – and you should be able to write about this. As part of your preparation, you could:

- apply the course contents to a non-profit making organization; for example, identify its "market", its "customers" and its "competitors"

- compare profit-making and non-profit-making organizations; for example, examine if marketing models may be applied in the same way

- read about famous leaders and managers of different types of organizations; explain why they have the same features and characteristics, no matter what the organization is.

QUESTION PRACTICE

This question refers to the May 2018 case study of Suchenlin and the two organizations she has founded, a travel agency called High-end Holidays (*HH*) and a social enterprise called Afghan Sun (*AS*). Su has appointed several managers to help her run these two organizations.

With reference to Su and her managers at *HH* and *AS*, explain the differences between leadership and management.   [6]

SAMPLE STUDENT ANSWER

Response 1

Leadership and management go hand-in-hand, both play a vital role within a business. Leadership tends to take the hands off approach as opposed to management, where they come face-to-face with the shortcomings and progression of the company. Leadership has an indirect role inside of the company while still remaining a key part to the success of the company. Management directly immerses themselves into the company. Management has a workload not only focusing on problems inside of the business but outside of the business as well. Repetitious communication takes place between management and leadership. New comings have to be reported to leadership, they have a xxx relationship.

> ▲ The candidate contrasts leadership and management, which shows some subject knowledge.

> ▼ The points made are valid (although rather abstract at times) but they are only theoretical, although the question started with the words "With reference to Su and her managers". The candidate unfortunately ignored that part of the question.

This response could have achieved 3/6 marks.

Response 2

One difference between leadership and management is that while leaders focus on the long-term plans of a business, managers handle the short- to medium-term issues that a business is facing. It is known that Su is not taking a part in the day to day running of HH and she has an input into the strategic decision making while her managers make day to day and tactical decisions.

> ▲ The first paragraph already shows that the candidate has understood the task well: contrasting leadership and management, with reference to Su and her managers. The first paragraph is about a first difference, well applied.

Another difference between is that leadership has a more emotional quality when it comes to inspiring workers towards a common goal while managers' responsibility is to direct subordinates. While Su "provides the inspiration for HH" and "the managers are inspired by Su", the managers direct staff with a more professional approach. With the ability to motivate and inspire others, Su, as a leader, helps workers and managers to understand her mission and get together for a common goal. The managers however, are more task-oriented.

> ▲ The second paragraph is about a second difference. The candidate quotes the case study, which is a good technique to substantiate their ideas. It is good to see that all through the answer, the candidate uses subject terminology, for example here using "task-oriented".

Another difference between leaders and managers is that while leaders are not afraid to take risks and welcome change, managers try to avert risks and apply the policies of the business they are working for. Su, as a leader, takes the risk of investing 200,000 into a new business when she already has enough money. The managers however, try to avert risks by coordinating and taking tactical decisions.

> ▲ Third paragraph, third difference – always with a balance of "theory" and "practice". The candidate also shows that they understand the story of the case study very well.

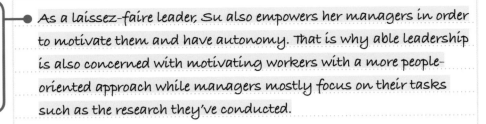

▲ Although the question is not explicitly about leadership styles, the candidate harnesses knowledge of leadership styles very well in their answer, showing the examiner that they master unit 2.3. The answer is clear and thorough.

As a laissez-faire leader, Su also empowers her managers in order to motivate them and have autonomy. That is why able leadership is also concerned with motivating workers with a more people-oriented approach while managers mostly focus on their tasks such as the research they've conducted.

This response could have achieved 6/6 marks.

>> Assessment tip

When you write long answers, it is good practice to set paragraphs. A paragraph is a coherent unit of meaning; with paragraphs, the layout of your answer shows your ability to structure your thoughts. In this last example, the candidate wrote four separate paragraphs, each corresponding to one of the differences between leadership and management. Not only is it more reader-friendly for the examiner, but it also shows the ability to organize ideas in a logical way, as opposed to writing one simple block of text with many ideas but no clear structure.

Test yourself

Explain how a good leader can also be a good manager, and how a good leader could also be a bad manager.

>> Revision tip

As you revise the course contents, it can be useful to work with pairs of opposite terms that you can contrast, for example "leadership versus management" or "democratic versus autocratic". The reality of business management in general, and of human resources in particular, is however more nuanced than this. In your exam answers, make sure that you can also demonstrate your critical thinking skills, especially to go beyond simple oppositions. For example, you could explain how the same person can be both a leader and a manager, or how someone can adapt their leadership style according to the situation, sometimes more democratic and sometimes more autocratic.

>> Assessment tip

In your extended responses (Sections C of SL paper 2, HL paper 1 and HL paper 2) you may want to refer to the leaders or managers of your chosen organization. Make sure that you know enough about them, especially the correct spelling of their names: the Austrian founder of Red Bull is Dietrich Mateschitz, and he was inspired by a Thai drink invented by Chaleo Yoovidhya. Criterion E is called "Individuals and societies" so you have to write about "relevant stakeholders, including individuals". Leaders and managers are individuals – it may be very good to mention them in your answer, as this may help you achieve a higher mark for Criterion E.

Content link
Link to other sub-units

- Sub-unit 2.2 examines organizational structure; this is closely linked to this sub-unit, as leadership and management style should fit the structure of the organization. For example, an autocratic leadership style would be more appropriate for a tall, centralized, bureaucratic organization than for a flat, decentralized organization.

- Sub-unit 2.4 explores the topic of motivation; this is closely linked to this sub-unit, as managers and leaders must find ways to motivate their employees.

- Sub-unit 2.6 (HL only) examines the relations between employees and employers, especially in cases of conflict; this is closely linked to this sub-unit, as many conflicts are due to management and leadership styles.

Concept link

All six concepts are linked to the topic of leadership and management:

- **Culture** has a direct impact on leadership and management: leaders and managers must respect and understand the culture of the organization where they work, especially if they have just been appointed externally. For cultural reasons, some employees may respond differently to different leadership styles: some employees may prefer paternalistic leaders, others may prefer democratic ones.

- **Ethics** plays an increasing role in leadership and management: leaders and managers are becoming more aware of the ethical dimensions of their actions and decisions. For example, feminism has helped raise male managers' awareness of some behaviour towards women that is not ethically acceptable any longer.

- Leaders and managers may need to **change** and adapt their style according to **changes** in the internal and external environment of the organization. For example, a leader who had a laissez-faire approach may need to become more autocratic if employees are underperforming and the organization's survival is at stake.

- How about **innovation, strategy** and **globalization**? How can you link these three concepts to the topic of leadership and management?

Content link
Link to your IA

Even if your IA is not specifically about human resources, you can apply the contents of this sub-unit to your chosen organization. How would you describe the managers' leadership styles? Why? And how appropriate are they? Would different styles be appropriate for the organization? Your IA gives you the chance to learn more about the contents of this sub-unit in context.

2.4 MOTIVATION

You should be able to:

✔ discuss the main ideas from five motivation theorists: Taylor, Maslow, Herzberg, Adams and Pink

✔ distinguish between the eight types of financial rewards

✔ distinguish between the six types of non-financial rewards

✔ explain how financial and non-financial rewards may affect job satisfaction, motivation and productivity in different cultures.

This sub-unit presents key ideas from five influential motivation theorists and explains how, in practice, employees can be rewarded and motivated, financially and non-financially.

Topic summary

Several **motivation theories** can help business managers understand the psychology behind workers' motivation (and demotivation):

- **Taylor**'s time and motion studies about efficiency and the standardization of working practices.

- **Maslow**'s pyramidal hierarchy of human needs (the more needs an employer can satisfy, the more motivated the employees will be).

- **Herzberg**'s basic "hygiene needs" (that must be satisfied) vs "true motivators".

- **Adams**' equity theory ("equity" between inputs and outputs).

- **Pink**'s model of Autonomy, Mastery and Purpose.

There are eight types of **financial rewards**:

1. **Salary** (usually paid monthly).

2. **Wages: time rates** (possibly with overtime rates of pay).

3. **Wages: piece rates**.

4. **Commission** (for example a flat fee or percentage for each item sold).

5. **Profit-related pay**.

6. **PRP: Performance-related pay** (usually a bonus).

7. **Employee share ownership schemes** (payment in shares of the business, or savings plan).

8. **Fringe payments (perks)** sometimes linked to the nature of business.

There are six types of **non-financial rewards**:

1. **Job enrichment** (making the job more meaningful and rewarding).

2. **Job rotation** (also common as a form of training).

3. **Job enlargement** (which can include job enrichment and job rotation).

4. **Empowerment** (giving employees control over how to do their job).

5. **Purpose** (the opportunity to make a difference, socially or environmentally).

6. **Teamwork** (working with colleagues to achieve a common goal).

Financial and non-financial rewards may affect job satisfaction, motivation and productivity in different cultures; all financial and non-financial rewards have different degrees of effectiveness in different countries and cultures. Some workers are mostly interested in making (more) money, whereas others may respond more to non-financial rewards. Managers must consider which rewards, or combination of rewards, are more suitable, depending upon the context.

Test yourself

Explain the main advantages and disadvantages of all the financial and non-financial rewards.

>> **Assessment tip**

How long should your answers be?

In business management, there is no specification about word count in exam answers. You should use three factors to help you estimate how long your answers should be, i.e. how much you should write to achieve a high mark:

1. **How many marks are allocated to the question?** For a question worth only 2 marks, you can answer in a few sentences, one paragraph at most.

2. **How much time are you expected to spend on the question?** In business management, the allocation is approximately 2 minutes per mark, so for a question worth 2 marks, you are only expected to spend 4–5 minutes. In fact, as these questions tend to be straightforward, you are likely to spend much less, thereby saving time for the longest, more demanding questions (worth 10 marks and 20 marks).

3. **What is the command term?** A straightforward command term such as "state" asks for a short answer (a few words may be enough) whereas an evaluative command term such as "discuss" implies a much longer answer with balanced arguments.

Examples:

Using Herzberg's motivation theory, explain one reason for the recent issue at TH with punctuality and absenteeism. [2 marks]	This question is only worth 2 marks, so keep your question short: a couple of sentences are enough. You do not need to write everything you remember about Herzberg's two-factor theory, such as the difference between what he calls "hygiene needs" versus "true motivators". Go to the point: the examiner expects a short answer combining "theory" (with a reference to Herzberg's ideas) and "practice" (the application to the case study: punctuality at TH in this case).
Apply Daniel Pink's motivation theory to the programmers at Gen Y. [6 marks]	This question is worth 6 marks, so your answer should be long and thorough; the examiner can expect you to spend around 10 minutes answering this question, where you must show: • that you know Pink's three key drivers (Mastery, Autonomy, Purpose) • that you can apply each, in turn, to the case study. Your answer is likely to be structured in three paragraphs, with each paragraph linking one of the three drivers to the case study (the programmers at Gen Y).

>> **Assessment tip**

Do not spend too much time on questions worth only 2 marks (even if you have a lot to write) and make sure you sufficiently develop your longer answers.

Sometimes, the question will ask you specifically which motivation theories to use, such as Herzberg and Pink in these examples – but sometimes you are free to choose yourself.

QUESTION PRACTICE

This question is about a hotel called Thorn Hills (*TH*) which is encountering problems of punctuality and absenteeism.

Using Herzberg's motivation theory, explain **one** reason for the recent issue at *TH* with punctuality and absenteeism. [2 marks]

SAMPLE STUDENT ANSWER

Response 1

The employees of TH Function Room are on flexible contracts that do *not* cover what Herzberg calls "hygiene needs": no job security, no guaranteed hours of work, decreasing relationship with supervisors (as a consequence of the de-layering). They express their lack of motivation through their absenteeism and lack of punctuality.

▲ The candidate shows their knowledge of Herzberg's hygiene factors and applies it well to the context of TH. This is a very good answer.

This response could have achieved 2/2 marks.

QUESTION PRACTICE

This question is about an internet start-up business called Gen Y Limited, owned by Zack Johnson. The employees are specialist programmers and coders who create innovative market research data reports.

Apply Daniel Pink's motivation theory to the programmers at Gen Y. [6 marks]

Gen Y programmers have <u>autonomy</u>, especially to work on their own "dream projects" one day a week (so 20% of their time); this autonomy goes with the fact that they are empowered to make their own decisions, which fits Zack's "laissez-faire" leadership style well.

Gen Y programmers have <u>mastery</u> – it is showed in their ability to be innovative (and intrapreneurs); they have also received cognitive training – to know how to take risks in their work, without stress and anxiety. They master their technical knowledge (programming) but other soft skills too – and they are clearly motivated by the job enlargement.

Gen Y programmers have <u>purpose</u>: the reports they write have "revolutionized Gen Y's clients' ability to understand and respond to customers in their markets" so the programmers must feel very proud – beyond making profit (which is actually the weak spot of Gen Y) they can see how their work is useful and contributes to other people's projects and the wider community.

▲ Each paragraph combines "theory" and "practice"; the candidate understands the three drivers (Autonomy, Mastery, Purpose) and applies them well to the case study with concise relevant examples. This is a very good answer.

This response could have achieved 6/6 marks.

This question is about a cleaning company called Green Clean (GC) whose cleaners are becoming demotivated, hence the question:

With reference to **two** motivation theories, examine the motivation of cleaners at GC.   [10]

How should you select the two motivation theories for your answer?

1. Choose motivation theories that you know well: for example, if you do not remember by heart the names and order of the levels in Maslow's pyramid of needs, do not choose it.

2. All five motivational theories may not be equally appropriate for the scenario given. The examiner will not penalize you for a poor choice, but it may make it harder for you to answer the question. In the case of GC cleaners, according to the stimulus material, the cleaners have always perceived their wages as fair. As a consequence, Adams' equity theory could be easily applied, especially if you consider the cleaners' feelings of unhappiness towards the newly appointed gardeners who have comparable skillsets but are paid much higher rates (hence a problem with the inputs/outputs equity). Pink's theory, however, may be harder to apply to the cleaners' motivation, especially as there is no reference to "autonomy" in the stimulus material.

If, in class, you have studied other motivation theories that are not in the IB syllabus (for example McGregor's Theory X and Theory Y or Vroom's expectancy theory), you may of course use them, you will not be penalized – though there is no expectation that you will know motivation theorists other than Taylor, Maslow, Herzberg, Adams and Pink.

Content link
Link to other sub-units

- Sub-unit 2.3 about leadership and management is closely linked to this sub-unit about motivation, because leaders and managers must ensure that their employees remain well motivated in order to perform well.

- Sub-unit 3.2 about costs has close links to this sub-unit about motivation as all financial forms of motivation represent a cost for the organization (sometimes a fixed cost, in the case of a salary; sometimes a variable cost, in the case of a commission or profit-related pay).

Concept link

All six concepts are linked to the topic of motivation:

- Employees' motivation may **change** over time; when it decreases (demotivation), managers may have recourse to different motivational techniques and rewards.

- Some organizations may decide to **innovate** in the way they motivate their staff: some employees may be more motivated by perks, others by the working conditions and what they may be allowed to do at their workplace, such as bring their pet dog, have a break when they want or dress informally.

- **Globalization** and **culture** pose challenges to the HR managers of MNCs, as workers in different countries will have different motivations and will respond differently to motivational techniques and rewards. Schemes that are successful in one country, for example performance-related pay, could be demotivating workers in another culture.

- How about **ethics** and **strategy**? How can you link these two concepts to the topic of motivation?

Content link
Link to your IA

Even if your IA is not specifically about human resources, you can apply the contents of this sub-unit to your chosen organization. What types of financial and non-financial rewards are used? Has it always been the case? Could there be sometimes problems of demotivation with some employees? What could cause this, and why? What could be done about it? Your IA gives you the chance to learn more about the contents of this sub-unit in context.

2.5   ORGANIZATIONAL (CORPORATE) CULTURE (HL ONLY)

This sub-unit focuses on the way organizations, like countries, have their own culture, with their own attitudes, beliefs and values.

You should be able to:

✔ define the term "organizational culture"

✔ explain the elements that make up the culture of an organization

✔ distinguish between types of organizational culture

✔ discuss how individuals influence organizational culture, and how organizational culture influences individuals

✔ discuss the reasons for, and consequences of, cultural clashes within organizations, when they grow, merge, and when leadership styles change.

Test yourself

Describe the culture of three different organizations that you have studied.

>> Assessment tip

It is rare to have an exam question *solely* on the topic of organizational culture; however you may need to refer to it when you answer other questions. Even if the term "organizational culture" is not explicit in the question, always think about it.

Topic summary

The term **organizational culture** (sometimes called **corporate culture**) refers to the attitudes, experiences, beliefs and values of an organization – and the way all employees interact with one another, and with external stakeholders.

The culture of an organization is made up of many elements, such as its history and traditions, symbols and language used, norms and expectations. Many theorists have written about organizational culture, for example Handy's typology of "power culture", "role culture", "task culture" and "person culture". The culture of an organization could be described as conservative (traditional), international, entrepreneurial, innovative, etc. Organizational culture can change, rapidly or not; individuals (such as a new CEO) may influence the culture of the organization, just as the organizational culture influences all employees.

Culture clashes happen for many reasons, such as different degrees of formality, different practices, different senses of time – and can lead to many problems, such as higher labour turnover, conflict and decreased productivity.

Content link
Link to other sub-units

Several sub-units are closely linked to this one:

* Sub-unit 1.6 about growth and evolution, as a merger will have an impact on the culture of the newly created organization (as the two companies merging may have different cultures, with the risk of culture clashes).

* Sub-units 2.1 and 5.2, as a new strategy of outsourcing or offshoring would have an impact on the culture of the organization.

* Sub-unit 2.2 about organizational structure, as a change in the structure of the organization may have an impact on its culture, especially if the structure becomes taller or flatter.

* Sub-unit 2.3 about leadership and management, as for example the external appointment of a new CEO may have an impact on the culture of an organization.

2.6   EMPLOYER AND EMPLOYEE RELATIONS (HL ONLY)

You should be able to:

✔ explain the role and responsibility of employee and employer representatives

✔ explain common sources of conflict at work

✔ evaluate the main methods of industrial relations used by employers and by employees (trade unions)

✔ discuss the main approaches to conflict resolution at work

✔ analyse reasons for resistance to change in the workplace

✔ discuss human resource strategies for reducing the impact of change and resistance to change

✔ discuss how innovation, ethical considerations and cultural differences may influence employer-employee relations in an organization.

This sub-unit focuses on the relations between employer and employee, especially regarding conflict and conflict resolution at work, as well as change management.

Topic summary

The relations between employers and employees (also called **industrial relations**) may sometimes be tense or difficult about the terms and conditions of employment, typically about pay, change taking place at work, different values and interests, insufficient resources and poor communication.

In larger organizations, employers and employees have **representatives** who are responsible for discussing and negotiating together in order to reach agreements and to avoid the creation and escalation of conflicts. These discussions are called **collective bargaining**. When collective bargaining is not successful:

- employees may go on strike, or may decide to "go slow", "work-to-rule" or refuse to work overtime

- employers may threaten employees with redundancy, with change of contract, or could close the workplace and lock the employees out.

Test yourself

Identify the advantages and disadvantages of the different types of action that may be taken by employees and by their employer, when collective bargaining fails and industrial dispute begins.

The main approaches to conflict resolution at work are:

- **conciliation and arbitration**, with the intervention of an independent third party

- **employee participation** and **industrial democracy**, involving employees more directly in decision-making, consultation or communication

- **no-strike agreement** by the trade union, so work will not completely stop

- **single-union agreement**, which means that the employer negotiates with only one trade union.

There are many reasons why employees may be against change, including fear, insufficient rewards, mistrust, negative prior experience, self-interest, low tolerance to change, misinformation and misinterpretation of the change and its rationale.

HR strategies for reducing resistance to change include robust planning and clear communication about the change, its intended outcomes and benefits. It is essential to manage change well, as it could otherwise lead to further conflicts and lower performance, harming the organization.

Innovation, ethical considerations and cultural differences may influence employer-employee relations in many ways, as for example the arrival of a new manager replacing one who had different values and cultural expectations could lead to conflict with workers not prepared for that change.

>> **Assessment tip**

Questions using the command term "define" are the only questions where you are *not* required to include examples or applications. They are always worth 2 marks, and you will score:

- 1 mark if you show *partial* knowledge and understanding of the term

- 2 marks if you show *good* knowledge and understanding of the term.

Example: Define the term "arbitration"

Response 1	Arbitration is a form of collective bargaining.	**Incorrect answer:** Arbitration is not a form of collective bargaining, it is an approach to conflict resolution. No mark can be awarded when the answer is not correct at all. **0 marks.**
Response 2	Arbitration is a method to resolve an industrial dispute when the employer and the workers cannot agree.	**Partial answer:** The candidate has some knowledge of what arbitration means, but an important idea is missing, about the intervention of the conciliator. **1 mark.**
Response 3	Arbitration is a method to resolve an industrial dispute when the employer and the employees cannot agree. It usually involves a neutral, independent third party who acts as conciliator and intermediary to help find a solution.	**Full answer:** The candidate's knowledge is good and correct. **2 marks.**

Although short answers may be comprehensive enough to be rewarded by 2 marks, it is always a good idea to develop your answer a little – and you have time to write more than one or two lines!

For your definitions, write a couple of sentences, or make two distinct points – that way, you show the examiner that your knowledge is sound and secure: if your answer is too short, you may give the impression that you do not know much (even if you do).

The examiner will reward your knowledge and understanding of the term, so do not worry if your definition feels a bit clumsy or not too elegantly formulated. Likewise, do not worry about spelling, grammar and punctuation; the examiner will not penalize you if you write "lockout" instead of "lock-out".

Content link
Link to other sub-units

- Sub-unit 2.3 about leadership and management is closely linked to this sub-unit because a manager's leadership style may be a source of conflict. For example, if an autocratic manager in a given department replaces one who had a more laissez-faire approach, the employees may be unhappy with the way they are now managed.

- Sub-unit 2.5 (HL only) about organizational culture is closely linked to this sub-unit because the culture of an organization influences industrial relations. Some companies may have a culture of recurrent dispute and conflicts between employer and employees, for example in the manufacturing sectors in some countries such as France.

- Sub-unit 5.7 (HL only) about crisis management is relevant as the most extreme cases of industrial conflict may require the organization to communicate to its stakeholders about what is happening.

Concept link

All six concepts are linked to the topic of employer and employee relations:

- The relations between employer and employees keep **changing** over time, from periods of harmony to episodes of open conflict; the aim of collective bargaining is to anticipate and avoid these conflicts.

- The **culture** of the country may influence the way trade relations are handled. In some countries, trade unions are virulent and vocal, whereas in others they have limited power or may not even exist.

- Open conflicts can be detrimental to the image of an organization, for example when customers are "victims" of workers who go on strike (e.g. flights or trains are cancelled). These conflicts may also harm business performance and financial results. In such cases, organizations need to have several **strategies** in place to ensure that they do not lose their customers: communication strategies, financial strategies, operational strategies.

- How about **ethics**, **globalization** and **innovation**? How can you link these three concepts to the topic of employer and employee relations?

 Content link
Link to your IA

Even if your IA is not specifically about human resources, you can apply the contents of this sub-unit to your chosen organization. Have there been cases of tension or even open conflict at work, with industrial action? How are the relations between employer and employees usually handled? How is change managed in the organization? Your IA gives you the chance to learn more about the contents of this sub-unit in context.

3 FINANCE AND ACCOUNTS

You should know:

- ✔ Sources of finance
- ✔ Costs and revenues
- ✔ Break-even analysis
- ✔ Final accounts (some HL only)
- ✔ Profitability and liquidity ratio analysis
- ✔ Efficiency ratio analysis (HL only)
- ✔ Cash flow
- ✔ Investment appraisal (some HL only)
- ✔ Budgets (HL only)

3.1 SOURCES OF FINANCE

This sub-unit focuses on the sources of finance available to businesses.

You should be able to:

- ✔ explain the role of finance, distinguishing between capital expenditure and revenue expenditure
- ✔ define short-term, medium-term and long-term finance
- ✔ distinguish between the three internal sources of finance: personal funds (for sole traders), retained profit, and sale of assets
- ✔ distinguish between the ten external sources of finance: share capital, loan capital, overdrafts, trade credit, grants, subsidies, debt factoring, leasing, venture capital, and business angels
- ✔ discuss the appropriateness, advantages and disadvantages of sources of finance for a given situation.

Topic summary

Finance has two roles, **capital expenditure** and **revenue expenditure**:

- Capital expenditure is long-term investment: money spent to acquire **fixed assets** in a business, such as machinery, equipment, vehicles, buildings.

- Revenue expenditure is money used for the day-to-day operations of a business, for example purchasing raw materials, paying wages and energy bills.

Sources of finance can be categorized as **short-term**, **medium-term** or **long-term**:

- Short-term finance should be paid back within 12 months, for example bank overdrafts and trade credit.

- Medium-term finance usually has a duration between one year and five years; it is typically for equipment or vehicles that have a specific lifespan; examples include leasing and grants.

- Long-term finance has a duration of 5 to 30 years; it is a long-term investment to purchase land or a building, for example a long-term bank loan or share capital.

There are three **internal** sources of finance:

1. **Personal funds**: sole traders often use their own savings, sometimes with external sources of finance, for example to show a bank their personal commitment.

2. **Retained profit**: for an existing business (as opposed to a new start-up), this is what remains after payment of tax (to the government) and dividends (to the shareholders); it can be described as a form of reinvestment and is also called "ploughed-back profit".

3. **Sale of assets**: when the business sells unwanted or unused assets (for example obsolete machinery or vehicles) to raise funds.

There are ten **external** sources of finance:

1. **Share capital** (also known as "equity capital"): money raised from the sale of shares of a limited company; public limited companies sell their shares on the stock exchange.

2. **Loan capital** (also known as "debt capital"): money from a financial institution, such as a bank; it is repaid in instalments with interest (at a fixed rate or at a variable rate).

3. **Overdrafts**: when a lending institution (such as a bank) allows a business to withdraw more money than it has on its account, for a short, temporary period of time.

4. **Trade credit**: an agreement between businesses that allows the buyer to pay the supplier later, after a period of time, such as one to three months.

5. **Grants**: funds provided by the government or other organizations such as foundations or agencies, often following a bid (application, proposal) which may be competitive.

6. **Subsidies**: a form of financial assistance, often from the government or non-governmental organizations (NGOs); they sometimes take the form of subventions and, like grants, do not have to be repaid.

7. **Debt factoring**: a financial arrangement with a "debt factor", i.e. a third business taking responsibility for collecting payment; it keeps a percentage of the owed debt as a payment for its services.

8. **Leasing**: a source of finance that allows a firm to use an asset without purchasing it, but renting it, with periodic payment.

9. **Venture capital**: capital provided by investors (such as investment banks, as opposed to high street banks) to high-risk, high-potential start-up enterprises or small businesses.

10. **Business angels**: rich individuals who invest in start-up enterprises in return for part-ownership and some control in its strategic development.

All sources of finance have advantages and disadvantages; they will be more or less appropriate for a given situation. When choosing a source of finance, several factors must be taken into consideration, especially:

- Duration (short-, medium-, or long-term).

- Source (internal or external).

- Amount required.

- Level of flexibility.

- Purpose.

QUESTION PRACTICE

Utopia is a resort on the island of Ratu in the Pacific Ocean. Paul, the son of the owner, is considering developing the brand of *Utopia* by selling customized souvenirs produced by three-dimensional (3D) printers, which would cost $10 000.

With reference to *Utopia*, describe two suitable sources of finance for the 3D printers.   [4]

SAMPLE STUDENT ANSWER

Response 1

▲ This short introduction is useful; the candidate displays some promising knowledge of the subject (sources of finance) and names the two sources of finance that they will develop in their answer: retained profit and bank loan.

> Sources of finance are used to kickstart a business, which are separated into internal sources of finance and external sources of finance. The new 3D printer business could utilize retained profits and bank loans as suitable sources of finance.

▲ The first source of profit is briefly defined, then then candidate goes on to apply it to the case study ("Connecting it to *Utopia*…")

> First or all, retained profits are the money that the business earned from their previous year's operations.

▲ The candidate uses subject terminology (e.g. "capital expenditure") throughout their answer, always applying it to the situation.

> Connecting it to Utopia, as the 3D printing business is an extension for Utopia, John and Paul could utilize profits earned from Utopia before the natural disaster to cover all the costs for the 3D printing business. For example, they could use retained profits to pay for the $10 000 needed for capital expenditure and still possess enough cash for the daily running of the business.

▲ The next part starts with a new paragraph, which makes the answer easy to follow.

▲ The candidate shows that they understand that all sources of finance have advantages and disadvantages, but they justify their answer, with reference to the case study.

> Furthermore, the 3D printing business could ask for loans from banks that could be paid back after one year in the balance sheet. Loans from banks would ensure that the 3D printing possessed enough finance for the business to continue running for one more year. However, the Ariki family would need to take into account the interest rates charged by the banks as they would need to make sure that they have enough money to pay back the loan.

Note: The answer is very clear and contextualized: 2 marks for each suitable source of finance, well described with reference to *Utopia*, as required by the task.

This response could have achieved 4/4 marks.

Assessment tip

As in this answer, use business management terminology throughout. Here, the candidate used terms such as "capital expenditure", "balance sheet" and "interest rates". This is the vocabulary of our subject: show the examiner that you know these terms and that you can use them accurately; this will help you score higher marks. The Grade 7 descriptor includes the following feature: "a precise use of terminology which is specific to the subject".

SAMPLE STUDENT ANSWER

Response 2

One suitable source of finance for the 3D printers could be the external investors/stakeholders that wish to see the brand develop and to increase profit. Since they function with Utopia's best interest in mind, out of the many external finance sources, costs could be covered quickly. Another suitable source of finance would be internal finances, since John refuses to grow any business through external finance, he can finance for 3D printers through retained profit, out of his own personal funds, loans and so on. Both of these finance sources would be a suitable option to fund the 3D printers.

▼ The first part of the answer is vague ("external investors/ stakeholders") and confusing: "stakeholders" are not a source of finance; maybe the candidate meant "shareholders" – but then they are not external.

▲ The second part of the answer includes the terms "retained profit" and "loans" which are two acceptable sources – even if the answer is a little confusing, as the candidate seems to consider them together, as one single source, but the examiner is giving the candidate the benefit of the doubt.

Note: Two suitable sources are identified overall (retained profit and loans), but not developed.

This response could have achieved 2/4 marks.

 Content link

Link to your IA

Even if your IA is not specifically about finance and accounts, you can apply the contents of this unit to your chosen organization. What sources of finance do they normally use? Why? Has it always been the case? Your IA gives you the chance to learn more about the contents of this unit in context.

 Content link

Link to other sub-units

- This sub-unit introduces unit 3 in general, so all other sub-units 3.2 to 3.9 are linked to it.
- Sub-units 3.1 and 1.1 are linked as an entrepreneur must identify their main sources of finance in the business plan.

Assessment tip

You may be asked about the suitability of a particular source of finance; use your critical thinking skills. For example, overdrafts would not be suitable to purchase a vehicle, but leasing would be.

Concept link

The concept of **change** is linked to the topic of sources of finance because a business will have access to different sources of finance over time. When they set up their business, many entrepreneurs use their personal funds; retained profit and sales of assets are not available at this point. Established organizations, on the other hand, have access to different sources of finance, such as retained profit (reinvestment) and equity capital.

3.2   COSTS AND REVENUES

This sub-unit examines the different types of costs paid by all organizations, and the revenue streams that help them determine their profit.

You should be able to:

✔ distinguish between the different types of costs

✔ explain how various revenue streams contribute to the total revenue of a business and therefore to its profit.

Topic summary

Costs can be:

- direct or indirect

- fixed or variable.

▼ Table 3.2.1 Costs overview

Direct costs	Costs linked to the production of specific goods and services (and thus to a specific "**cost centre**").	Examples: raw materials, direct labour, packaging costs.
Indirect costs	Costs that cannot be linked to the production of goods and services – also called "**overheads**".	Examples: rent, general administrative expenses, insurance, maintenance, cleaning and security.
Fixed costs	Do not change with the amount of goods or services produced.	Examples: rent/mortgage, insurance, salaries, interest payments.
Variable costs	Change with the amount of goods or services produced.	Examples: raw material costs, sales commission, packaging, energy usage costs.

Some costs are composed of both fixed and variable elements; they are called "**semi-variable costs**" (or "semi-fixed costs" or "mixed costs") – for example in the case of a reward package composed of "fixed salary + overtime" or "fixed salary + commission".

Total costs (TC) = total of fixed costs (TFC) + total of variable costs (TVC)

The main **revenue** of a business is usually the income from its trading activities, i.e. the income gained from the sale of goods and services, also called "sales revenue", "sales turnover", "turnover". It is calculated by multiplying the price per unit by the quantity of goods sold.

The **total revenue** of a business could have other streams (components):

- Rental income (the income from renting its properties, maybe seasonally).

- Sale of fixed assets (especially if they are unused or underused).

- Dividends (if it owns shares in another business).

- Donations, grants, subsidies.

>> **Assessment tip**

In daily language, many people talk about **revenue** and **profit** as being the same – but they are not:

- Revenue is the money generated by the sale of goods and services.

- Profit is calculated by total revenue minus total costs (TC).

The revenue of a business might be very high, but if the costs are very high too, the business might not be profitable!

Another common mistake is to mix the terms **cost** and **price**:

- Cost is the expense incurred for a product sold by a company (it includes direct and indirect costs, from the purchase of raw materials and direct labour, to contribution to overheads such as insurance, cleaning and security).

- Price is the amount charged to the customer (it may be calculated from the cost itself, for example with a mark-up, or using a different pricing strategy, for example based on competitors' prices).

When you use these words in your answers to business management exam questions, be careful.

Test yourself

State examples of costs that are:

- direct and variable

- direct and fixed

- indirect and variable

- indirect and fixed.

>> **Assessment tip**

Common questions about this unit tend to use the command term "define", such as:

Define the term *variable* costs. [2]

Someone who has never studied business management might simply say "costs that vary" – but in a business management exam, this is not enough. In your answer, you must be more technical, stating that the variation depends on the level of output.

Content link

Link to your IA

Even if your IA is not specifically about finance and accounts, you can apply the contents of this unit to your chosen organization:

- What are its main streams of revenue? Have they changed over time? Could you suggest one more possible stream of revenue for the organization?

- What are its main costs centres?

Your IA gives you the chance to learn more about the contents of this sub-unit in context.

 Content link

Link to other sub-units

- Sub-units 3.2 and 3.3 are closely linked because fixed costs and variable costs play a key role in the calculation of break-even.

- Sub-units 3.2 and 3.7 are closely linked because costs and revenue are key elements in a cash flow.

- Sub-units 3.2 and 4.5 are closely linked, because costs and prices are often wrongly taken as synonymous; the calculation of costs is explained in 3.2, whereas the setting of prices is explained in 4.5.

Concept link

The concept of **change** is linked to the topic of costs and revenues because costs and revenue streams are all subject to change. By nature, variable costs change according to the level of output, whereas fixed costs do not. Revenue also changes, according to the volume of sales and other factors (e.g. discounts) which means that profit always fluctuates too.

3.3 BREAK-EVEN ANALYSIS

You should be able to:

✔ distinguish between "contribution per unit" and "total contribution"

✔ draw a break-even chart with the break-even quantity/point (BEQ/BEP)

✔ calculate the break-even quantity, profit, margin of safety, target profit output, target profit and target price

✔ explain the effects of changes in price or cost on the break-even analysis, profit and margin of safety, using graphical and quantitative methods

✔ discuss the benefits and limitations of break-even analysis.

This sub-unit focuses on break-even analysis, an important model that helps a company calculate and see at what point it starts making profit.

Topic summary

The **contribution** shows how much a product contributes to the fixed costs and thus to the overall profit of a business, after deducting the variable costs:

(1) **Contribution per unit = price per unit – variable cost per unit**

The contribution per unit is needed to calculate the break-even point.

(2) **Total contribution = total revenue – total variable costs**

Total contribution can also be calculated with this formula:

Total contribution = contribution per unit × number of units sold

After establishing the total contribution, profit can then be calculated:

Profit = total contribution – total fixed costs

Profit = (contribution per unit × number of units sold) – total fixed costs

Which corresponds to:

Profit = total revenue – total variable costs – total fixed costs

Profit = total revenue – total costs

The **break-even quantity** is the minimum number that must be sold so that all costs are covered by revenues. At the **break-even point**, there is no loss, but no profit either.

They can be calculated **numerically or graphically**, on a **break-even chart**.

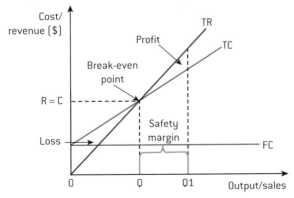

▲ Figure 3.3.1 A break-even chart with margin of safety

The break-even quantity can be calculated in two ways:

1. Using the "contribution per unit" method:

$$\text{Break-even quantity} = \frac{\text{Fixed costs}}{\text{Contribution per unit}}$$

2. Using the "total costs = total revenue" method.

Once the break-even point is reached, it is said that the company is "breaking even" – and it then starts making profit. This is called the **margin of safety**.

Margin of safety = current output – break-even output

Based on the break-even quantity formula, two other calculations are possible:

$$\text{Target output profit} = \frac{\text{Fixed costs + target profit}}{\text{Contribution per unit}}$$

$$\text{Break-even revenue} = \frac{\text{Fixed costs}}{\text{Contribution per unit}} \times \text{price per unit}$$

On the break-even chart, it is possible to observe the effect of changes in price or costs, especially how an increase in fixed costs or in variable costs pushes the break-even quantity higher, with a decrease in the margin of safety.

Break-even analysis has several advantages (for example: the chart is easy to use and interpret) but also disadvantages (for example: it assumes that all costs and revenue lines are linear, which is not always the case, for example with price reductions or discounts).

>> **Revision tip**

Questions about break-even are asked frequently, especially in Section A of paper 2, so make sure you know how to answer questions about break-even. There is an element of mathematics because business management has a quantitative dimension, which is why the Section A of a paper is always about quantitative analysis.

QUESTION PRACTICE

Moverse

Moverse operates in the health and fitness sector. *Moverse* is not a traditional gym with machines (equipment) and fitness instructors (trainers). The instructors themselves travel and run fitness classes in the buildings of large companies. Instructors all work part-time and are paid wages on a time rate basis.

Moverse currently sells its services to several large companies. They have a total of 727 employees enrolled on its programme.

- *Moverse* charges a yearly fee of $145 for each employee participating.
- *Moverse*'s fixed costs are $60 000 per year.
- The variable cost per employee taking part in the programme is $45.

a) Calculate the break-even quantity for *Moverse* (*show all your working*). [2]

b) Construct a fully labelled break-even chart, to scale, for *Moverse* if 800 employees enrol on *Moverse*'s training programme. [4]

c) Calculate the profit or loss if 800 employees enrol on *Moverse*'s training programme (*show all your working*). [2]

a) Break-even quantity = 60 000/145−45 = 600

BEQ = 600 employees

This response could have achieved 2/2 marks.

▲ The break-even quantity is calculated by dividing the total of fixed costs ($60 000) by the contribution per unit (selling price of $145 per employee participating minus $45 variable cost per employee participating). The candidate remembers and applies the formula well.

≫ Assessment tip

When you read such a stimulus, the main difficulty is to identify different elements. In order to calculate the contribution per unit, ask yourself "what is the unit?" In this case, the unit is the employee taking part in the fitness programme, hence the final answer written: the BEQ (break-even quantity) is 600 "employees" as "units".

b)

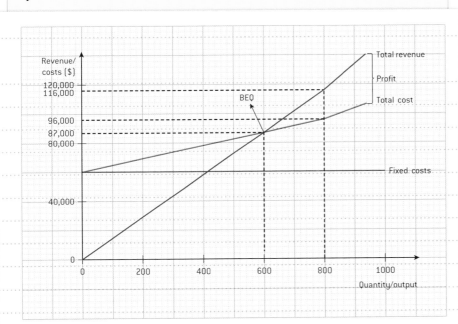

Note: All the aspects assessed are correct:

* The chart is fully labelled.

* All the lines are accurately drawn.

* The break-even point is correctly placed.

This response could have achieved 4/4 marks.

≫ Assessment tip

Do not forget to label the break-even chart fully, with the axes and lines. Some marks are always awarded for this; these marks are easy to achieve. But they are also easy to miss out on, if you forget to add the labels and the names of the different elements. Likewise, you should use graph paper, provided by your school for the exam, or use your ruler.

c) Total revenue = 800 × 145 = 116 000

Total costs = 60 000 + (800 × 45) = 96 000

Profit = total revenue – total cost = 116 000 – 96 000

$$= 20\,000$$

▲ The answer is correct and the candidate showed their workings (i.e. they did not just write the final answer ($20 000)).

● Profit = $20 000

This response could have achieved 2/2 marks.

≫ Assessment tip

There are two ways to calculate profit. The candidate used the formula:

Profit = total revenue – total variable costs – total fixed costs

The alternative was to use the formula:

Profit = total contribution – total fixed costs

i.e.

Profit = (contribution per unit × number of units sold) – total fixed costs

So in this case:

Contribution per unit = 145 – 45 = $100

Profit = (100 × 800) – 60 000 = 80 000 – 60 000 = $20 000

It does not matter which method you choose. Once you have obtained your result, it is worth spending a couple of minutes to double check your result, using the other method. You will be reassured if both answers match, or you will be able to spot that you made a mistake and then correct it.

≫ Assessment tip

Make sure you understand the difference between **contribution** and **profit**, as some candidates mix them up:

- Contribution is the difference between the sales prices and the variable costs of a product; this then contributes to the fixed costs and goes towards the profit of the business.

- Profit is the difference between sales and all costs (both variable costs and fixed costs). It is the total revenue minus all the costs. If the costs are higher than the sales revenue, the result is "a negative profit", i.e. a loss.

Content link
Link to other sub-units

- Sub-units 3.3 and 3.2 are closely linked because the fixed and variable costs explained in 3.2 play a key role in the calculation of break-even.

- Sub-units 3.3 and 3.4 are closely linked because the trading account (the first part of the income statement) starts with the calculation of profit as sales revenue minus costs of sales, all elements introduced in 3.3.

Concept link

The concept of **change** is linked to the topic of break-even analysis because the break-even chart shows how changes in price or costs have an impact on break-even quantity and profit.

Content link
Link to your IA

Even if your IA is not specifically about finance and accounts, you can apply the contents of this unit to your chosen organization: do they use break-even methods? Why/why not?

3.4 FINAL ACCOUNTS (SOME HL ONLY)

You should be able to:

✔ discuss the purpose of accounts to different stakeholders

✔ examine the principles and ethics of accounting practice

✔ prepare and interpret:

  ✔ the profit and loss account (P&L account) of a business

  ✔ the balance sheet of a business

✔ define "intangible assets"

✔ calculate depreciation (HL only) using two methods (straight line and reducing balance)

✔ explain the strengths and weaknesses of each method (HL only).

This sub-unit focuses on two types of financial statements used by businesses: profit and loss accounts (P&L) and balance sheets.

Topic summary

Numerous stakeholders need to know the financial statements of a business:

- Shareholders, because the dividends they receive is calculated from the profit and loss account.

- The government, because the profit and loss account helps to calculate the taxes that the business will have to pay.

- Potential investors and financiers, because they will want to know about the creditworthiness and financial health of the business to decide how much they can invest in it.

- Managers, because final accounts help them monitor performance, comparing the results to previous years, and set budgets and strategies.

- Employees, because a profitable business means that their job is secure, or that they could get a pay rise.

Ethics in accounting is the study of moral values and judgments applied in the accounting process. Accountants should follow "codes of ethics" – with principles such as honesty, objectivity and confidentiality.

The **profit and loss account** (also called **income statement**) shows the records of income and expenditure over a period, typically a year. It includes data (such as **gross profit** and **net profit**) and eventually indicates if the business has made a **profit** or a **loss**. In the case of a profit, it shows how this profit is distributed (e.g. payment of **dividends** to shareholders, or **retained profit**).

The **balance sheet** indicates the assets, liabilities and equity of a firm at a specific date.

- The **assets** are what the company owns: **fixed assets** (long-term, such as buildings or vehicles) and **current assets** (lasting less than a year: stock/inventory, current cash, and money owed by debtors).

- The **liabilities** are what the company owes: **long-term liabilities** (such as a bank loan) and **current liabilities** (short-term debts to be paid within a year, money owed to creditors, tax payable to the government).

The balance sheet makes it possible to calculate the **working capital** ("net current assets") of a business:

Working capital = total current assets – total current liabilities

Another important calculation is the net assets of a business:

Net assets = total assets – current liabilities – long-term liabilities

The net assets correspond to the **equity** of a business, indicating how the assets were financed (**share capital** from shareholders and **retained profit**).

Besides the "fixed assets" and "current assets" of a business, there is a third type of "assets": **intangible assets**. These are not physical, cannot easily be quantified and showed on a balance sheet, even though they add value to a business. The main examples of **intangible assets** are trademarks, patents, goodwill and copyright.

Depreciation (HL only) is the decrease in the value of a fixed asset over time.

The two main reasons for depreciation are:

- Wear and tear (for example for vehicles or machinery, as their repeated use means that their value decreases and more money is needed to replace them).

- Obsolescence (for example computer hardware and software that fall in value as new or improved values are introduced in the market).

This is recorded in the profit and loss account as an expense. It can be calculated in two ways:

(1) Using the **straight line method**. This method is commonly used as it is simple to calculate. The cost is equally spread over the lifetime of the asset, using the following formula:

$$\text{Annual depreciation} = \frac{\text{Original cost} - \text{residual value}}{\text{Expected life of asset}}$$

Every year, it is the same amount which is counted as annual depreciation expense.

(2) Using the **reducing balance method**, applying a percentage depreciation rate over the lifetime of the asset (always the same percentage rate).

Net book value Year 1 = Cost of original asset – (cost of original asset × percentage rate of depreciation)

The following table gives a comparison for the depreciation of the same asset, a vehicle initially worth $30 000 (its net book value):

▼ Table 3.4.1 Comparison for the depreciation of the same asset

Year	Straight line depreciation		Reducing balance depreciation	
	Annual depreciation expense	Net book value	Reducing balance with annual rate of 33%	Net book value
0	0	$30 000	0	$30 000
1	$6000	$24 000	$9 900 (30 000 × 33%)	$20 100
2	$6000	$18 000	$6 633 (20 100 × 33%)	$13 467
3	$6000	$12 000	$4 444 (13 467 × 33%)	$9 023
4	$6000	$6 000	$2 977 (9 023 × 33%)	$6 046

Both methods have advantages and disadvantages, for example the straight line method is simple to calculate but may initially inflate the value of some assets; the reducing balance method is more realistic but more complex.

>> **Revision tip**

Questions about final accounts are asked very often. There is usually *at least one* in each exam, so make sure you know how to approach these questions. It is essential that you know the exact order of the elements in the two final accounts (profit and loss; balance sheet). The IB has specific presentation requirements for these accounts; you must learn them and follow them. There are other presentation methods in some books, and some national systems are slightly different too.

>> **Assessment tip**

Questions about final accounts usually only require you to provide numbers and tables, unless you are also asked to interpret the data, i.e. to write some text to explain what they mean.

QUESTION PRACTICE

Sotatsu Electronics (SE)

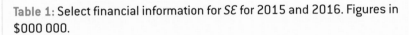

Sotatsu Electronics (SE) manufactures electronic products and is famous for its innovative televisions. In late 2015, *SE* introduced a new high-definition television with twice the quality of the best-selling television of its chief competitor. Determining that it would be two years before its competitors could have a similar product, *SE* adopted a price skimming strategy.

Table 1: Select financial information for *SE* for 2015 and 2016. Figures in $000 000.

	2015	2016
Cash	300	250
Cost of goods sold	2100	2300
Creditors	180	230
Expenses	1200	1300
Fixed assets	1075	1275
Gross profit	**X**	2800
Net profit before interest and tax	1000	**Y**
Sales revenue	4300	5100
Total current assets	650	700
Total current liabilities	275	300

(...)

a) **i)** Calculate the values of **X** and **Y** in Table 1 (*no working required*).
[2]

   ii) Construct a profit and loss account for *SE* for 2015 **and** 2016. [4]

b) Calculate net current assets (working capital) for 2016 (*show all your working*).
[2]

▲ The results are correct. The candidate included the workings (i.e. the details of how they did their calculations). This was not necessary, it would have been enough to write the values of **X** and **Y**.

Assessment tip

Remember to add the unit at the end. This is very important for all your calculation results: $2 200 is not the same as 2 200 or 2 200%.

SAMPLE STUDENT ANSWER

a i)

X = Gross profit in 2015

Gross profit = sales revenue – costs of goods sold = 4300 – 2100

= 2200

X = $2 200 000 000

Y = Net profit before interest and tax in 2016

Net profit before interest and tax = gross profit – expenses

Net profit before interest and tax = 2800 – 1300 = 1500

Y = $1 500 000 000

This response could have achieved 2/2 marks.

SAMPLE STUDENT ANSWER

a ii)

	2015	2016
Sales revenue	4300	5100
Costs of goods sold	2100	2300
Gross profit	2200	2800
Expenses	1200	1300
Net profit before interest and tax	1000	1500

(All figures in $000 000)

Note: The profit and loss accounts are correct.

This response could have achieved 4/4 marks.

b)

Working capital = total current assets – total current liabilities

700 – 300 = 400

Net current assets (working capital) in 2016 = $400 000 000

▲ The result is correct – and this time, the workings *were* required.

This response could have achieved 2/2 marks.

QUESTION PRACTICE

Geo Dynamics (GD)

Geo Dynamics (GD) is an engineering company. On 1 January 2016, *GD* purchased new machinery at a cost of $50 000 rather than leasing it. *GD*'s financial manager researched further information:

- The machinery has a useful life of four years.

- Its residual or scrap value will be $8000.

- The engineering industry uses a 40% depreciation rate per annum.

- Technology in this industry is changing rapidly.

GD's financial manager has not yet decided on which depreciation method (such as straight line or reducing/declining balance) to use for the new machinery.

a) Calculate the value (also known as net book value) of new machinery at 31 December 2017 using the straight line depreciation method (*show all your working*). [2]

b) Calculate the value (also known as net book value) of new machinery at 31 December 2017 using the reducing/declining balance method, applying the industry depreciation rate of 40% per annum (*show all your working*). [4]

c) Explain **one** advantage for GD of using the straight line balance depreciation method. [2]

SAMPLE STUDENT ANSWER

a)

$$\text{Annual depreciation} = \frac{\text{purchase cost} - \text{residual value}}{\text{Life span}}$$

$$\frac{50\,000 - 8\,000}{4} = 10\,500 \text{ per year}$$

$10\,500 \times 2 = 21\,000$

$50\,000 - 21\,000 = 29\,000$

By the end of 2017, it will have a book value of $29\,000

Note: This answer is correct.

This response could have achieved 2/2 marks.

b)

Year	Depreciation	Net book value
At the beginning of 2016	0	50 000
At the end of 2016	(50 000 × 40%) = $20 000	50 000 – 20 000 = $30 000
At the end of 2017	(30 000 × 40%) = $12 000	30 000 – 12 000 = $18 000

Note: The answer is correct. The candidate did not include the formula, but this was not required – they showed their workings and they clearly know how to calculate the reducing balance method.

This response could have achieved 4/4 marks.

c) An advantage is the fact that the higher amount of depreciation in the first year is more realistic, as machinery and vehicles usually lose more value in the early years than later on.

This response could have achieved 0/2 marks.

▼ The candidate wrote about an advantage of the reducing balance method, not an advantage of the straight line method! It may be because they just calculated depreciation using the reducing balance method and had this in mind. Although the answer shows knowledge and understanding, well applied here, they cannot score any marks, as they did not answer the question asked, but another one.

Content link
Link to other sub-units

- Sub-units 3.4 and 3.5 are closely linked because some of the data in the final accounts make it possible to calculate profitability and liquidity ratios.

- Sub-units 3.4 and 3.6 (HL only) are closely linked because some of the data in the final accounts make it possible to calculate efficiency ratios.

Content link
Link to your IA

Even if your IA is not specifically about finance and accounts, you can apply the contents of this sub-unit to your chosen organization. Ask if you can see their P&L accounts and their balance sheets. Their financial statements may be more complicated than the models used here, and the terminology may be slightly different, but the principles are the same. You could also ask if they calculate the depreciation of some of their fixed assets over time, and how they do it. Your IA gives you the chance to learn more about the contents of this sub-unit in context.

Concept link

The concept of **ethics** is linked to the topic of final accounts because accountants should have a high standard of ethics. The ACCA (Association of Chartered Certified Accountants), the international body for professional accountants, has a "Code of Ethics and Conduct" which is binding for all its members who must commit themselves to follow the five principles of integrity (honesty), objectivity, professional competence, confidentiality and professional behaviour.

3.5   PROFITABILITY AND LIQUIDITY RATIO ANALYSIS

This sub-unit focuses on five financial ratios calculated from financial statements.

You should be able to:

✔ calculate and interpret two profitability ratios: the gross profit margin and the net profit margin

✔ calculate and interpret one efficiency ratio: ROCE

✔ discuss possible strategies to improve these ratios

✔ calculate and interpret two liquidity ratios: current ratio and acid-test/quick ratio

✔ discuss possible strategies to improve these ratios.

Topic summary

The two **profitability ratios** help assess the performance of a business based on its ability to generate profit. They use data from the profit and loss account.

Gross profit margin (GPM)

$$\text{Gross profit margin} = \frac{\text{gross profit}}{\text{sales revenue}} \times 100$$

Net profit margin (NPM)

$$\text{Net profit margin} = \frac{\text{net profit before interest and tax}}{\text{sales revenue}} \times 100$$

Several strategies may help improve GPM, for example increasing prices (to increase sales revenue) or trying to find cheaper suppliers (to decrease the cost of goods sold). To improve NPM, the business could also try to reduce expenses (for example overheads).

The **efficiency ratio ROCE** helps measure how well a business utilizes its assets and liabilities. It uses data from the balance sheet to assess the returns a business is making from its capital employed.

$$\text{Return on capital employed (ROCE)} = \frac{\text{net profit before interest and tax}}{\text{capital employed}} \times 100$$

Capital employed = long-term liabilities + share capital + retained profit

Several strategies may help improve ROCE, for example the business could pay more dividends to shareholders, reducing the retained profit and thus increasing ROCE.

The **liquidity ratios** measure the ability of a business to pay off its short-term debts, i.e. how quickly current assets could be converted into "liquid" cash. They use data from the balance sheet.

Current ratio

$$\text{Current ratio} = \frac{\text{current assets}}{\text{current liabilities}}$$

Acid test (quick) ratio

$$\text{Acid test (quick) ratio} = \frac{\text{current assets} - \text{stock}}{\text{current liabilities}}$$

As a rule of thumb, these ratios should be around 1.5. Low ratios (under 1) mean that the business could struggle to pay off its debts. High ratios (above 2) should be avoided too, as they could mean that there is too much cash being held unnecessarily and not invested, or that there are too many debtors. These numbers, however, vary across industries and are related to speed of stock turnover: retail, for example, may not need as high a current ratio or acid test ratio.

Several strategies may help improve the liquidity ratios. The business could try to increase current assets and/or decrease current liabilities, or both. Selling off the stock at a discount is another possibility

---

QUESTION PRACTICE

AFA was at a critical point. Sam and Finn had not fully resolved their disagreements. They seemed to be constantly arguing but Sam could also see that new issues were emerging. At their most recent meeting in early 2018, Finn provided the following financial information to illustrate the declining trend in gross profit margin.

Table 1: Selected financial information for *AFA*

Year	Gross profit	Sales revenue
2016	142 888	2 164 486
2017	124 211	2 400 625

(…)

a) **i)** Calculate the gross profit margin of *AFA* for 2016 **and** 2017. [2]

ii) Explain one possible reason for the trend in gross profit margin for *AFA* between 2016 and 2017. [2]

SAMPLE STUDENT ANSWER

Remember to add the percentage sign at the end of the GPM, NPM and ROCE, otherwise you would not achieve top marks, even if your calculation is numerically correct. The percentage sign is an integral part of your answer; it shows that you understand that a ratio is a proportion, expressed as a percentage.

▼ The candidate does not answer the question about a possible reason. They repeat the numbers that they have just calculated and comment on the fact that it is a negative indicator, but this is not the question asked. To achieve some marks, the candidate should have commented on a likely cause: the fact that direct costs have risen faster than sales revenues (that have increased).

SAMPLE STUDENT ANSWER

a) i)

$$GPM\ 2016 = \frac{142\,888}{2\,164\,486} \times \frac{100}{1} = 6.6\%$$

$$GPM\ 2017 = \frac{124\,211}{2\,400\,625} \times \frac{100}{1} = 5.17\%$$

Note: The two results are correct.

This response could have achieved 2/2 marks.

ii) Gross profit margin went down between 2016 and 2017, from 6.6% down to 5.12%, which is not a good sign, especially as the text states that it is a trend.

This response could have achieved 0/2 marks.

 Revision tip

Calculating ratios is an important skill, but make sure that you also understand what these ratios mean, what information they provide, how they can be interpreted and how they can help a business to make decisions.

 Content link
Link to other sub-units

Sub-units 3.5 and 3.4 are closely linked because the profitability and liquidity ratios are calculated from data found in the final accounts.

 Content link
Link to your IA

Even if your IA is not specifically about finance and accounts, you can apply the contents of this sub-unit to your chosen organization. If you can have access to their profit and loss account and their balance sheet, do some calculations to practice your ratio calculation skills. Try to interpret your results, bearing in mind that all ratios must be interpreted in context.

Concept link

The concept of **change** is linked to the topic of profitability and liquidity ratios because ratio analysis only becomes meaningful when you compare changes and trends over several years, and across companies in the same sector. A ratio on its own does not mean much; for example, it is not possible to say if a gross profit margin of 10% is good or bad. This number must be compared to the gross profit margin of the previous years and to the gross profit margin of other businesses in the same sector in order to interpret it.

3.6 EFFICIENCY RATIO ANALYSIS (HL ONLY)

You should be able to:

✔ calculate and interpret four other efficiency ratios:

1) the stock (inventory) turnover ratio

2) the debtor (trade receivable) days ratio

3) the creditor days ratio

4) the gearing ratio

✔ discuss possible strategies to improve these ratios.

This sub-unit focuses on four other efficiency ratios calculated from the balance sheet.

Topic summary

Besides **ROCE**, there are four other efficiency ratios that help assess how well a business uses its resources, assets and liabilities:

1. The **stock (inventory) turnover ratio** that measures how quickly the stock is sold and replaced. It may be calculated in two ways: how many times a year, or how many days it takes to replenish the stock:

$$\text{Stock turnover (number of times)} = \frac{\text{cost of goods sold}}{\text{average stock}}$$

or

$$\text{Stock turnover (number of days)} = \frac{\text{average stock}}{\text{cost of goods sold}} \times 365$$

There are several strategies to improve stock turnover ratio, such as adopting a "JIT" (Just in Time) production method.

2. The **debtor ("trade receivable", "debt collection") days ratio** about the number of days it takes a business to collect its debts from the customers who have paid on credit, and thus owe money to the business.

$$\text{Debtor days ratio (number of days)} = \frac{\text{debtors}}{\text{total sales revenue}} \times 365$$

There are several strategies to lower debtor days ratio, such as giving incentives to debtors to pay their debts early, or fining late payers.

3. The **creditor days ratio** about the number of days it takes a business to pay its own debts to its creditors (e.g. typically to its suppliers).

$$\text{Creditor days ratio (number of days)} = \frac{\text{creditors}}{\text{cost of goods sold}} \times 365$$

Possible strategies to increase creditor days ratio include negotiating extra time with suppliers ("trade credit").

4. The **gearing ratio** measures the extent to which the capital employed by a business is financed from loan capital. Put another way, this is the level of debt of a business. A "highly geared" business (with a ratio of 50% or above) is seen as risky by financiers.

$$\text{Gearing ration} = \frac{\text{loan capital}}{\text{capital employed}} \times 100$$

capital employed = loan capital (or long-term liabilities) + share capital + retained profit

Possible strategies to reduce gearing ratio include seeking sources of finance other than a loan, for example issuing more shares.

QUESTION PRACTICE

Bart Furniture (BF)

Bart Furniture (BF) is a wholesaler that stocks furniture. In 2015, BF purchased more stock than usual in order to take advantage of discounts that several furniture manufacturers were offering. However, much of this new stock did not sell.

Table 1: Financial information, for *BF*, for 2015 and 2016

	2015	2016
Acid-test/quick ratio	2.21	2.84
Cash	$2000	$500
Cost of goods sold	$12 166	$12 500
Creditors	$1000	$1438
Current ratio	**A**	5.47
Debtor days	30 days	**Y**
Debtors	$1973	$6134
Long-term debt	$14 000	$13 700
Sales revenue	$24 000	$26 000
Short-term debt	$800	$900
Stock	$4000	$6164
Stock turnover in days	**X**	180

(…)

a) Using information in **Table 1**, calculate for *BF*:

   i) stock turnover in days for 2015 (**X**) (*show all your working*);   [2]

   ii) debtor days for 2016 (**Y**) (*show all your working*).   [2]

SAMPLE STUDENT ANSWER

a) i)

$$\text{stock turnover} = \frac{\text{Average stock}}{\text{costs of goods sold}} \times 365$$

$$\frac{4000}{12166} \times 365 = 120$$

Note: The answer 120 is numerically correct but the candidate did not include the unit "days".

This response could have achieved 1/2 marks.

ii)

86 days

Note: The answer is numerically correct, but the candidate did not show their working, though this was required.

This response could have achieved 1/2 marks.

>> Revision tip

For questions about efficiency ratios, you need to use data from the balance sheet, so make sure you understand the elements of a balance sheet well, including their exact order. The IB has specific presentation requirements for the balance sheet, which may be slightly different from the balance sheet in your country and in some of your books. You must learn and follow the IB presentation of the balance sheet.

 Content link

Link to your IA

Even if your IA is not specifically about finance and accounts, you can apply the contents of this unit to your chosen organization. If you can have access to their balance sheet, do some calculations about their efficiency ratios and try to interpret your findings, bearing in mind that all ratios must be interpreted in context.

Content link

Link to other sub-units

- Sub-units 3.6 and 3.4 are closely linked because the efficiency ratios are calculated from data found in the balance sheet.

- Sub-unit 3.6 and 5.5 are linked because one of the strategies to improve stock turnover ratio is the product method JIT (just-in-time) explained in 5.5.

- Sub-unit 3.6 and 3.1 are linked because one of the strategies to increase creditor days ratio is trade credit, i.e. an agreement with suppliers to pay them later, as defined in 3.1, and strategies to reduce gearing ratio include seeking sources of finance other than a loan, for example issuing more shares, also defined in 3.1.

Concept link

The concept of **change** is linked to the topic of efficiency ratios because these ratios, like the other financial ratios, are only meaningful when you take the context into account, the norms in the sector and the evolution of the ratios over a period of time: ratio analysis is all about observing how ratios change, interpreting these changes, drawing conclusions and formulating recommendations for the business.

3.7   CASH FLOW

This sub-unit focuses on an important financial planning tool: cash flow forecast.

You should be able to:

✔ distinguish between profit and cash flow

✔ analyse the working capital cycle

✔ construct and interpret cash flow forecasts

✔ analyse the relationship between investment, profit and cash flow

✔ discuss strategies to deal with cash flow problems to improve these ratios.

Topic summary

Profit is the positive difference between sales revenue and total costs; it includes *both* cash transactions *and* credit transactions.

Cash flow is money that flows in and out of a business over a given period of time; it *only* includes cash transactions, not credit transactions. Insolvency is when a business runs out of cash, even though it may still be profitable: it is a problem of liquidity crisis without enough cash to run the day-to-day operations.

The **working capital cycle** is the period of time between payment of goods supplied to a business and receiving cash from their sale. It should be as short as possible because cash only ceases to be tied up at the end of each cycle, and profit is released when goods are sold and revenues received.

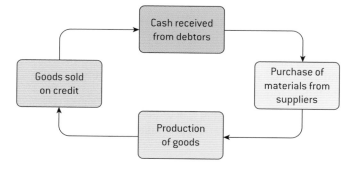

▲ Figure 3.7.1   A simple working capital cycle

A **cash flow forecast** is a financial document in the form of a table that shows the predicted cash inflows and cash outflows, for example month by month:

▼ Table 3.7.1 Cash flow with typical items of inflow and outflow as well as closing balance

	Month 1	Month 2	Month 3	Month 4
Opening cash balance	X	Y	Z	
Cash inflows				
– Cash sales revenue				
– Payment from debtors				
– Borrowing from bank				
– Rental income				
– Sale of assets				
Total cash inflows	A			
Cash outflows				
– Raw materials				
– Wages, salaries				
– Electricity				
– Rent				
– Marketing expenses				
– Purchase of fixed assets				
– Paying creditors				
– Repaying loans				
– Paying dividends				
Total cash outflows	B			
Net cash flow	A – B			
Closing balance	Y = X + (A – B)	Z		

Note: This example is a monthly cash flow, however each period could be shorter or longer, for example days or quarters.

The relationship between investment, profit and cash flow varies at different stages of a business. A new business usually requires a lot of investment (to purchase the first fixed assets) but there is no profit yet, and cash flow is negative. An established business, on the other hand, requires less investment, but achieves more profit, with a positive cash flow.

There are three main strategies to deal with cash flow problems:

- **Reducing cash outflow** (for example delaying the purchase of some fixed assets, delaying payment of suppliers or sourcing cheaper suppliers).

- **Improving cash inflows** (for example not allowing delayed payment on credit).

- **Looking for additional finance** (for example selling some assets and leasing them back).

Cash flow forecasts have several advantages. Like budgets, they are useful planning tools, providing estimated projections. They cannot however take into account unexpected changes in the economy, or in competitors' strategies.

Anubis

Tom operates *Anubis* as a sole trader, selling cell/mobile phone cases on the internet. The market is increasingly competitive. The retail price of phone cases is predicted to fall in the second quarter of 2018. Employees at *Anubis* will receive a 3% rise in wages starting from 1 April 2018.

Tom has forecasted the following monthly cash outflows for January through March 2018:

- Heating and lighting: $4000.
- Wages: $50 000.
- Packaging: $15 000.
- Delivery charges: 5% of sales revenue.
- Cost of goods sold: $220 000.

Additional information:

- Opening balance on 1 January 2018: $8000.
- Sales revenue: $300 000 each month.
- Rent of $2000 paid quarterly: first payment in January 2018.
- Receipt of a tax refund in February 2018: $3000.

(…)

a) Using the information above, prepare a fully labelled cash flow forecast for *Anubis* from January to March 2018.   [5]

b) Comment on the predicted cash flow for *Anubis* for 2018.   [3]

a)

	January	February	March
Opening balance	8000	2000	1000
Inflows:			
Sales revenue	300 000	300 000	300 000
Tax refund		3000	
TOTAL INFLOWS	300 000	303 000	300 000
Outflows:			
Electricity	4000	4000	4000
Wages	50 000	50 000	50 000
Packages	15 000	15 000	15 000
Costs of goods sold	220 000	220 000	220 000
Delivery charges	15 000	15 000	15 000
5% of sales revenue			
Rent	2 000		
TOTAL OUTFLOWS	306 000	304 000	304 000
NET CASH FLOW	−6000	−1000	−4000
Closing balance	2000	1000	3000

▼ There is one error at the end, when the candidate calculated the closing balance for March: it is a negative closing balance of −3000 (minus 3000). The omission of the minus sign is very important in cash flow forecasts! It looks like the candidate calculated 4000 − 1000 = 3000 instead of 1000 − 4000 = −3000

Note: The table is good overall, the candidate clearly understands key principles of a cash flow forecast.

This response could have achieved 4/5 marks.

b) The cash flow forecast is worrying because the opening balance keeps decreasing, which is not a good indicator. Based on the trend of January, February and March, the following months will probably be worse. Wages in April will be higher (+3%) and there will also be rent to pay again, so with more cash outflows, April will be a difficult month for Anubis.

This response could have achieved 2/3 marks.

▲ The candidate rightfully interprets that, overall, the cash flow forecast is a cause for concern, and they make some valid points about the ongoing trend and what will happen in April.

▲ For an even higher mark, the answer should be even more developed, for example noting that the business faces lower gross profit margin, and that action is necessary to deal with the impending cash flow problems, for example reducing cash outflows, maybe on packages by finding cheaper suppliers (the packages represent 5% of sales revenue, which is a lot).

≫ Assessment tip

Questions about cash flows are asked often, so make sure you know how to approach them. In most cases, you will be given a list of facts and data and asked to construct a table. You could also be given a cash flow forecast for a given period, for example a few months, and asked to prepare the cash flow forecast for the months that follow. You must remain vigilant though: the transactions are not the same every single month, for example some expenses may take place quarterly (every three months), or there might be a delay in cash flows in or out, for example with credit and debit terms. Go through all the information very slowly, when you construct your cash flow forecast.

≫ Assessment tip

Cash flow and profit are different financial parameters that some candidates (and some business owners!) mix up. Make sure that you understand the difference and that you use the terms correctly. Positive cash flows are not profits. Profit is the difference between sales revenue and all costs (i.e. all expenses), whereas a positive cash flow simply means that more cash went in than out. A business can have a positive cash flow and yet *no profit* if the cash comes from sources other than income, for example if they receive a bank loan, or if the owner puts some of their own money into the business. These transactions will be inflows in a cash flow table, however they are not income from sales revenue; they will appear as liability in the balance sheet.

⮌ Content link
Link to other sub-units

- Sub-units 3.7 and 3.2 are linked as cash flow is linked to costs and revenue streams.
- Sub-unit 3.7 and 3.4 are linked final accounts and cash flow forecasts should be read and interpreted together, as they offer complementary information about financial aspects of the business.

⮌ Content link
Link to your IA

Even if your IA is not specifically about finance and accounts, you can apply the contents of this unit to your chosen organization. What type of cash flow forecast do they use? It may be more elaborate than the simple model used here, but the principles are the same.

3.8 INVESTMENT APPRAISAL (SOME HL ONLY)

This sub-unit focuses on quantitative techniques used to evaluate the viability and attractiveness of an investment proposal.

You should be able to:

✔ calculate and evaluate investment opportunities using payback period and average rate of return (ARR)

✔ calculate and evaluate investment opportunities using net present value (NPV) (HL only).

Topic summary

Investment is the act of spending money to purchase a **fixed asset** with the expectation of future earnings. Investment appraisals are techniques that can help with deciding the suitability of an investment opportunity: financially, can the expenditure be justified? These techniques are also useful to compare competing investment opportunities. They can be combined to help decision-making.

The **payback period** refers to the length of time required for an investment project to pay back its initial cost outlay. It is expressed in years and months.

$$\text{Payback period} = \frac{\text{Initial investment}}{\text{Annual cash flow from investment}}$$

The payback period method has several advantages, especially the fact that it is simple and fast to calculate. It also has disadvantages, especially the fact that it ignores the overall profitability of an investment beyond its payback.

The **average rate of return (ARR)**, also called "accounting rate of return", measures the annual net return of an investment, as a percentage of its capital cost.

$$\text{Average rate of return (ARR)} = \frac{(\text{total returns} - \text{capital cost}) \div \text{year of use}}{\text{capital cost}} \times 100$$

The ARR method has several advantages, such as the fact that it shows the profitability of an investment project over a given period of time, allowing comparisons with other investment projects. It has disadvantages too, such as the fact that it does not consider the timing of cash inflows.

The **net present value (NPV)** is the difference between:

- the summation of present values of future cash inflows (returns), calculated using "discount factors" ("discount rates") provided in a "discount table" (in order to convert future cash flows into their present value)

- the original cost of the investment.

Net present value (NPV) = ∑ present values of return − original cost

The NPV method has several advantages, such as the fact that it takes opportunity cost and time value of money into account. It has disadvantages too, such as the fact that it is based on discount rates that may not be well predicted.

>> **Assessment tip**

Questions about investment appraisals are asked often, so make sure you know how to approach them. Typically, you are given a scenario and you are asked to apply investment appraisal techniques. As they all have advantages and disadvantages, you may be asked to recommend the most suitable one, depending on the scenario and the organization.

QUESTION PRACTICE

S4U is a private limited company that provides a storage facility to households and small businesses. *S4U* is considering constructing an additional new warehouse.

S4U's management has forecasted the following annual net cash flows for the new warehouse:

Year	Net cash flows ($)
0	−150 000
1	25 000
2	30 000
3	35 500
4	37 000
5	39 800
6	41 200

(…)

a) For the new warehouse:

i) using information from the table above, calculate the average rate of return (ARR) (*show all your working*); [2]

ii) using information from the table above, calculate the payback period (*show all your working*); [2]

iii) using information from the table below, calculate the net present value (NPV) at a discount rate of 6% (*show all your working*). [2]

Years	Discount rate
	6%
1	0.9434
2	0.8900
3	0.8396
4	0.7921
5	0.7473
6	0.7050
7	0.6651
8	0.6271
9	0.5919
10	0.5584

b) Explain **one** disadvantage for *S4U* of using the NPV method of investment appraisal. [2]

a) i)

Total returns – capital cost = 208 500 – 150 000 = 58 500

58 500 / 6 = 9750

9750 / 150 000 = 0,065

ARR = 0,065 x 100 = 6,5 %

▲ The result is correct. The candidate duly showed their workings, even though they could be slightly clearer.

This response could have achieved 2/2 marks.

ii)

Year 0	0	
Year 1	25 000	25 000
Year 2	30 000	55 000
Year 3	35 500	90 500
Year 4	37 000	127 500
Year 5	39 800	167 300

Year 4 and x months

39 800 / 12 = 3316 per month

150 000 – 127 500 = 22 500

22 500 / 3316 = 6,7

Payback period = between Year 4 and 6 months and Year 4 and 7 months

▲ The result is correct, even though other methods would have been possible, especially using a formula.

This response could have achieved 2/2 marks.

iii)

Year 1	25 000	0.9434	23 585
Year 2	30 000	0.8900	26 700
Year 3	35 500	0.8396	29 805.8
Year 4	37 000	0.7921	28 119.55
Year 5	39 800	0.7473	29 742.54
Year 6	41 200	0.7050	29 046
TOTAL			166 998.89

166 998.89 rounded up to 167 000

NPV = 167 000 – 150 000 = $17 000

▼ This is not the correct total. The candidate made an arithmetic error in one of the calculations.

▲ The correct answer is 18 188 so this is not correct, however the candidate clearly understands the principles of NPV, so may score 1 mark.

This response could have achieved 1/2 marks.

b)

The NVP method depends on the choice of the overall discount rate (6% here) and of the national interest rates for each year in the discount. There is no clear reason for the choice of 6%; if they choose another rate, the NVP results will be different.

> ▲ The answer is concise but clear; the candidate clearly understands one of the disadvantages of the NVP method.

This response could have achieved 2/2 marks.

≫ Assessment tip

Do not forget the units: payback in years and months, ARR as a percentage and NPV as a price!

Content link

Link to your IA

Even if your IA is not specifically about finance and accounts, you can apply the contents of this unit to your chosen organization. Do they use investment appraisal methods like the ones covered here?

Content link

Link to other sub-units

- Sub-units 3.8 and 3.7 are linked because there is a close relationship between investment, profit and cash flow.

- Sub-units 3.8 and 5.6 are linked because research and development often lead to the decision to invest in a new project, in a new venture.

Concept link

The concept of **strategy** is linked to the topic of investment appraisal because investment appraisal helps decide if a particular business venture is worth pursuing – or not. This can be a strategic decision for the organization, as it may have an impact on the goals they had initially set. For example, an investment in new machinery could prove too expensive, and the intended strategy of product development may consequently not be achievable.

3.9 BUDGETS (HL ONLY)

This short sub-unit focuses on a quantitative planning tool frequently used by all organizations: budgeting.

You should be able to:

✔ explain the importance of budgets for organizations

✔ state the difference between cost centre and profit centre

✔ analyse the role of cost centres and profit centres

✔ calculate and interpret variances in a budget

✔ analyse the role of budgets and variances in strategic planning.

Topic summary

Budget

A **budget** is a quantitative financial plan that estimates the revenue and expenditure over a future time period. The **budget holder** is the person responsible for the formulation and achievement of a budget.

Budgets are important for many reasons: they help in planning and setting targets, in allocating resources, in motivating budget holders, in controlling how funds have been spent.

Cost and profit centres

Cost centres are the sections of a business where costs are incurred and recorded, for example by item (wages, electricity, insurance), by department (marketing, production), by project, or by product. **Profit centres** are the sections of a business where both costs and revenues are incurred and recorded, usually by product line, or product.

Cost centres and profit centres have several roles: they provide information that can aid decision-making, improving accountability, tracking problem areas and benchmarking. Comparison between profit centres is not always easy and could lead to problems such as conflicts or staff stress, as the pressure of managing a budget may be high for some staff.

Variances

In budgeting, **variance** is the difference between the budgeted figure and the actual figure. It is calculated at the end of the budget period; it can be "favourable" (when the difference between the budgeted and actual figure is financially beneficial to the firm, for example spending less than anticipated) or "adverse" (when the difference between the budget and actual figure is financially costly to the firm, for example spending more than planned).

Strategic planning

Budgets and variance analysis play several roles in strategic planning. They help control revenue and expenditure, setting targets in line with the organization's strategic objectives. They also have limitations, as setting budgets without involving some people could result in their resentment and affect their motivation levels.

>> Assessment tip

You could be asked two types of question about budgets:

1 Quantitative questions.

2 Qualitative questions.

Quantitative questions will ask you to calculate something, usually variances:

Complete the variance column in the table below and establish whether the results obtained are adverse (A) or favourable (F).   [6 marks]

$000	Budgeted figure	Actual figure	Variance
Sales revenue	500	420	
Direct labour costs	50	50	
Direct material costs	80	90	
Gross profit	370	280	
Overheads	100	95	
Net profit	270	185	

Budgeted and actual figures for company *ABC Ltd* this year

Qualitative questions will require your answer to be in the form of written text, for example:

Define the term "variance analysis".   [2 marks]

Explain the importance of budgets to company *ABC Ltd.*   [4 marks]

Comment on the performance of company *ABC Ltd* using the variance results.   [6 marks]

Content link
Link to other sub-units

- Sub-units 3.9 and 3.7 are linked because budgets and cash flow forecasts have many similarities, although there are some differences, for example budgets do not have an "opening balance" and a "closing balance".

- Sub-units 3.9 and 2.3 are linked because budgeting (creating a budget) and monitoring budgets (analysing variances) are an essential responsibility of managers.

Content link
Link to your IA

Even if your IA is not specifically about finance and accounts, you can apply the contents of this unit to your chosen organization. Do they use budgets? Do they have systems of "cost centres" and "profit centres"? Do they do variance analysis?

Concept link

The concepts of **strategy** and **change** are linked to the topic of budgeting because strategic planning involves deciding how to allocate resources in order to achieve set objectives. Budgets however cannot consider unforeseen changes in the external environment, such as increase in the costs of raw materials, or negative competitive conditions. Budgets therefore should need to allow for timely revisions, or to take these changes into consideration when analysing adverse variance.

4 MARKETING

You should know:

- ✔ The role of marketing
- ✔ Marketing planning (including introduction to the four Ps)
- ✔ Sales forecasting (HL only)
- ✔ Market research
- ✔ The four Ps (product, price, promotion, place)
- ✔ The extended marketing mix of seven Ps (HL only)
- ✔ International marketing (HL only)
- ✔ E-commerce

4.1 THE ROLE OF MARKETING

This sub-unit introduces key terms, ideas and principles about the role and importance of marketing, one of the four business functions.

You should be able to:

- ✔ define marketing and its relationship to the other business functions
- ✔ distinguish between the following terms:
  - ✔ "marketing of goods" versus "marketing of services"
  - ✔ "market orientation" versus "product orientation"
  - ✔ "commercial marketing" versus "social marketing"
- ✔ describe the characteristics of the market in which an organization operates
- ✔ calculate market share
- ✔ discuss the importance of market share and market leadership
- ✔ compare and contrast the marketing objectives of for-profit and non-profit organizations
- ✔ discuss how marketing strategies evolve as a response to changes in customer preferences
- ✔ discuss how innovation, ethical considerations and cultural differences may influence marketing practices and strategies in an organization.

Topic summary

Marketing may be defined in many ways: it is about identifying and satisfying customers' needs; it is about getting the right product to the right customers at the right price at the right time.

Marketing of goods is about Product, Price, Place and Promotion (the four Ps); **marketing of services** takes three other aspects into consideration: People, Physical evidence and Process (the seven Ps). All these terms start with the letter P in English, which makes it easier to memorize.

A **market orientation** starts with market research first, in order to identify a market and its needs; a product will then be conceived and sold to this specific market. This is different from **product orientation** which focuses first on the product.

Commercial marketing aims at selling goods and services, whereas **social marketing** aims at influencing people and to change their attitudes, values or behaviour.

A market can be described in different ways:

- By size, either in volume (units) or in value (revenue).

- By growth rate (growth is the percentage change in total market size over a period of time).

Market share is the percentage of one company's share of the total sales in the market:

$$\text{Market share \%} = \frac{\text{Company's sales}}{\text{Total sales in the market}} \times 100$$

Market share can be measured by value (revenue) or volume (units); it is always expressed as a percentage. It makes it possible to identify the **market leader**, the company with the highest market share, which can be a brand leader and influence both competitors and customers.

The **marketing objectives** of profit-making organizations are geared towards profitability and income maximization, whereas non-profit organizations have social marketing objectives; because of their limited budget, they often have recourse to internet marketing.

Marketing strategies must evolve as a response to changes in customer preferences in order to ensure they remain relevant for their customers. Innovation, ethical considerations and cultural differences influence marketing practices and strategies in an organization in several ways, as marketing must fit the values of both the organization (internal stakeholders) and its customers (external stakeholders).

>> Revision tip

To help you consolidate your learning, you could identify examples of:

- Organizations that have a product orientation. Why is it suitable for them, as opposed to a market orientation?

- Organizations that are doing social marketing. How different is it from commercial marketing?

- Organizations that are market leaders. How did they become a market leader?

QUESTION PRACTICE

AS is a new social enterprise that is going to manufacture and sell solar power systems in Afghanistan. David, the marketing director, believes that commercial marketing would have more impact than social marketing.

With reference to *AS*, explain the difference between commercial marketing and social marketing of the solar power systems.   [4]

SAMPLE STUDENT ANSWER

Response 1

Commercial marketing is using mainstream marketing strategies to meet the wants and demands of a market. David believes this would have more of an impact than social marketing.

Social marketing is using mainstream marketing strategies to change social behaviours. Although David believes commercial marketing is better, a combination of both would be suitable as social marketing changes social behaviour and is a social enterprise which intends to give back to society.

▼ The second sentence does not add value to the answer ("David believes this would have more of an impact than social marketing") as this is just copied from the question.

▼ The final part of the answer (with the reference to social enterprise) does not answer the question about the difference between commercial marketing and social marketing

Note: Partial answer: the candidate can briefly define "commercial marketing" and "social marketing". However, they do not explain the difference between them, and yet that was the question!

This response could have achieved 2/4 marks.

Response 2

The main difference between commercial marketing and social marketing is the people it targets.

▲ The question is "Explain the difference" and right from the start the candidate states what the difference is, in their own words ("the people it targets").

Commercial marketing is about the narrow group of customers who will buy the solar panels. Commercial marketing is about influencing them to buy the panels, for example with promotional messages about the advantages to create electricity in their own home.

▲ The candidate explains the meaning of "commercial marketing" in the context of the case study (with the reference to the solar panels).

Social marketing is about the whole society of Afghanistan, not only AS customers, but everyone because everyone will benefit, especially in the poor and remote communities.

▲ The candidate explains the meaning of "social marketing" in the context of the case study (with the reference to Afghanistan).

Social marketing is not just about AS selling panels and making money, like commercial marketing, but about the long-term sustainable benefits for everyone, as in the actions of NGOs to make a change and improve society.

▲ The sentence is a "mini conclusion" that summarizes the difference, contrasting "commercial marketing" and "social marketing".

The solar power systems are product oriented and not market oriented. AS does not need to do market research to find out if there is a demand; they know there is a need for solar power systems to generate electricity in Afghanistan, so a commercial approach is fine.

▲ The last paragraph about product orientation and market orientation is not directly relevant, though the final sentence justifies why David prefers a commercial marketing approach.

Note: The answer is clear and in context. The candidate shows that they understand the difference and they apply the answer to the case study.

This response could have achieved 4/4 marks.

Content link
Link to your IA

Even if your IA is not about marketing, you can apply the contents of this sub-unit to your chosen organization. What role does marketing play in the organization? Do they have a product orientation or a market orientation? How would you describe the market where they operate? How would you evaluate their position in this market, compared to their competitors, based on their respective market shares? The organization you chose for your IA gives you the chance to learn more about the contents of this sub-unit in context.

Content link
Link to other sub-units

- This sub-unit introduces unit 4 in general, so all other sub-units 4.2 to 4.8 are linked to it.

- Sub-units 4.1 and 5.2 are linked as the choice of production method may depend on the organization's marketing approach (for example job production suits market orientation).

Concept link

The concepts of **culture, ethics** and **strategy** are linked to the role of marketing:

- **Culture** because marketers must pay close attention to cultural factors, especially cultural differences (for example in Israel, McDonald's offers kosher burgers, and in India more vegetarian ones).

- **Ethics** because businesses should consider their ethical responsibilities to promote their products accurately, to protect their customers and to take their wellbeing into account. (For example, how ethical is it to market products that may damage people's health?)

- **Strategy** because marketing has a strategic role in all organizations, irrespective of their type (commercial or non-profit); marketing has a cost, but it will ultimately lead to income generation, so it can be regarded as a strategic investment.

4.2 MARKETING PLANNING (INCLUDING INTRODUCTION TO THE FOUR Ps)

You should be able to:

✔ describe the elements of a marketing plan

✔ analyse the role of marketing planning

✔ explain the four Ps of the marketing mix

✔ construct and interpret an appropriate marketing mix for a particular product or business

✔ evaluate the effectiveness of a marketing mix in achieving marketing objectives

✔ distinguish between the terms:

    ✔ "market segments" and "target markets"

    ✔ "niche market" and "mass market"

This sub-unit introduces key terms and ideas about marketing such as the importance of marketing planning, perception maps and the four Ps of the marketing mix.

- ✔ identify possible target markets and market segments in a given situation
- ✔ analyse how organizations target and segment their market and create consumer profiles
- ✔ construct and interpret a product position map (perception map)
- ✔ explain the importance of having a unique selling point/ proposition (USP)
- ✔ discuss how organizations can differentiate themselves and their products from their competitors.

Topic summary

A **marketing plan** is a detailed document which includes marketing objectives and marketing strategies, as well as marketing activities (for example promotional campaigns) and the budget allocated to them. **Marketing planning** is the process of setting marketing objectives and devising strategies and tactics to meet these objectives. It has several advantages, for example sharing the marketing plan with other departments ensures that the whole organization knows what the marketing objectives are. Marketing plans can however be rapidly outdated.

The **four Ps of the marketing mix** are:

- Product – a good or service.
- Price – the amount customers are charged.
- Place – channels of distribution, how and where customers can get the product.
- Promotion – how potential customers are informed.

An **appropriate marketing mix** ensures that consumers' needs and wants are adequately met. It must be clear, coherent and focused, communicating to the right customers with the right message.

Market segmentation is the process of dividing a market into small groups, called **market segments**: sub-groups of consumers with similar characteristics. Markets can be segmented in different ways, using factors such as demographics (age, gender, religion, family characteristics, sexual orientation), geography (country, region, rural/ urban) or psychographics (social and economic status, values) in order to create typical **consumer profiles**.

Market segmentation helps businesses to identify the **target markets** they want to sell to, and to differentiate products and marketing activities according to these target markets. A **niche market** is a small and narrow market segment, whereas a **mass market** is a large, broad market segment. **Niche marketing** (also called concentrated marketing) is a strategy that only targets a specific niche market, whereas mass marketing (also called undifferentiated marketing) targets the entire market.

Product positioning is the analysis of how consumers perceive a product, compared to its competitors. It is usually represented with a diagram called a **position map** (or **perception map**) where the vertical and horizontal axes represent two variables, usually price and quality. Position maps are also useful to help identify gaps or opportunities in the market.

The **USP** (unique selling point, unique selling proposition) is what differentiates a product from its competitors. Having a USP is important to get **competitive advantage** and to ensure consumer loyalty. The four Ps of the marketing mix can constitute a USP.

QUESTION PRACTICE

Sam is a young entrepreneur. He wants to set up a retail store (AFA) selling fair trade chocolate, but he had insufficient funds. He has written a marketing plan for a local bank manager who is offering young entrepreneurs the chance to seek business finance and advice.

Describe **two** elements of a marketing plan for AFA. [4]

Response 1

Sam created a marketing plan for a local bank manager who was offering young entrepreneurs the chance to seek business finance and advice. In this the two elements of marketing plan are the finance and advice, in which the finance could be the way in which Sam will confront the problems of a business in the financial part.

▼ Finance is not applied to marketing: the candidate does not describe what this means in a marketing plan.

Also the advice, the enthusiasm he has to set up a retail store, the ideas he has in which he wants to put a business to sell chocolates.

▼ "Advice" and "enthusiasm" are not elements of a marketing plan; the candidate may be thinking about entrepreneurship and the business idea, this might be relevant for a business plan, but not for a marketing plan.

Note: Only the idea of "finance" can be credited here.

This response could have achieved 1/4 marks.

Response 2

Place: AFA sells its products at pop-up stalls which are temporary retail venues. So, actually Sam doesn't have enough funds, therefore use them can be a good idea because pop-up businesses are flexible and agile.

▼ The candidate refers to the marketing mix, with "place" and "price". It is true that the marketing mix may be included in a marketing plan, but in this answer, the two terms "place" and "price" are not well described.

Price: AFA doesn't have enough funds, so Sam could add a little mark up for balance his economy and sustain the business.

This response could have achieved 1/4 marks.

Response 3

One element of a marketing plan would be the marketing budget of the company. As can be seen from the case study, Sam had insufficient funds, hence planning the marketing budget of the company would allow for them to find out how much the company needs for advertisements and thus plan out the costs for the business.

▲ Budget is a correct answer: the marketing plan must include a budget, and the candidate explains that it is necessary to have a budget to cover the costs of advertising.

▼ Objectives is a correct answer, however the candidate does not refer to the marketing objectives of the company; the answer seems to be rather about a business plan in general, not a marketing plan focusing on marketing.

A second element of a marketing plan would be the objectives and strategies of the company. As can be seen from the case study, the marketing plan is for a local bank manager offering young entrepreneurs the chance to seek business finance and advice, hence the presence of the objectives and strategies of the company allows them to attract and motivate more young entrepreneurs as the young entrepreneurs would be able to learn more about the business.

Note: The answer is satisfactory. The first element is well described, with a reference to the budget for the advertising, but the second element about objectives is too generic, and not sufficiently about marketing.

This response could have achieved 3/4 marks.

>> Assessment tip

The questions about marketing are often the ones where many candidates underperform, because marketing may wrongly seem very easy. Candidates have a tendency to write "common sense" answers; they forget that marketing is an academic subject with a technical vocabulary that they should use in exam answers (for example about target market, USP and differentiation).

QUESTION PRACTICE

Describe **one** characteristic of a niche market.   [2]

Note: Niche markets can be defined as being small and narrow – but writing such a short definition is not enough to achieve two marks. The question asks you to describe one characteristic; the command term "describe" means give a detailed account. To be detailed enough to achieve two marks, your answer must be longer, for example:

SAMPLE STUDENT ANSWER

▲ The characteristic is well described. It is good to see how the candidate uses marketing terminology for example "consumer profile" and "mass market'.

A characteristic of a niche market is its very small size. A niche market is well defined and differentiated. It is small and narrow and the consumers have specific needs and wants. They share many features in their consumer profile, within the larger "mass market" of all consumers.

This response could have achieved 2/2 marks.

QUESTION PRACTICE

Davenport Electronics (DE)

Davenport Electronics (DE) is a small company that manufactures remote control electronic devices that open garage doors. The devices are kept in owners' cars. For years, *DE* devices operated in a fashion similar to those of its three competitors.

The three competitors are all larger than *DE*.

	Price of remote control	**Quality perception**
Company A	High	Medium
Company B	Medium	Medium
Company C	Low	Medium
DE	Medium	High

Using the table, construct a product position map/perception map for all four companies.   [4]

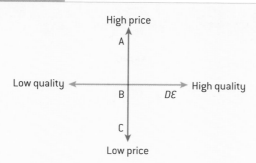

Note: The position map is correctly labelled and the four companies are correctly placed. The axes could have been presented differently (quality vertical and price horizontal).

This response could have achieved 4/4 marks.

>> Assessment tip

If you are asked to construct a perception map, you do not need to write any text: just draw the diagram but remember to label the axes; in this case, the horizontal one (x-axis) is quality, and the vertical one (y-axis) is price. These are the most common labels, but in other cases, it could be cost, budget, efficiency, style etc.

Content link

Link to your IA

Even if your IA is not about marketing, you can apply the contents of this sub-unit to your chosen organization. What are their main targets? Could you draw a perception map for one of their main products? Do they have a USP? How do they differentiate themselves from their competitors?

Content link

Link to other sub-units

- Sub-units 4.2 and 1.5 are closely linked because 1.5 introduces terms such as "strategic objectives" and "tactics" which are also relevant for marketing.

- Sub-units 4.2 and 4.5 are closely linked because 4.5 further explains the fours Ps of the marketing mix, going into more details.

Concept link

The concepts of **culture** and **strategy** are linked to the topic of marketing planning:

- **Culture** because market segmentation is often based on consumers' cultural characteristics (for example, a vegan restaurant will primarily target non-meat eaters).

- **Strategy** because marketing planning is not only about short-term decisions (for example about decorating a shop window to attract passing trade into the shop) but also about longer-term objectives (for example about setting objectives such as increasing sales by 5%).

4.3 SALES FORECASTING (HL ONLY)

This short sub-unit presents quantitative methods to identify trends in sales and to predict future sales.

You should be able to:

✔ calculate moving averages, plot sales trends including seasonal, cyclical and random variation and prepare sales forecasts

✔ discuss the benefits and limitations of sales forecasting.

Topic summary

Sales forecasting is important for several reasons. It aids the management of stock and cash flow, it helps make informed marketing decisions about pricing and promotion.

Time series analysis predicts future sales levels from past sales levels, identifying trends, patterns and variations. These variations can be:

- **Seasonal** – regular changes in demand at different times of the year (for example with a peak before Christmas).

- **Cyclical** – linked to the business cycle in the country's economy (for example with a recession).

- **Random** – unpredictable changes as anomalies in the time series (for example a very mild winter resulting in unusual demand for ice cream).

Calculating **moving averages** helps smooth out fluctuations from sales data by mapping trends over several years. It is then possible to extrapolate, i.e. to extend the trend line to predict future sales.

- Calculating a three-year moving average simply means calculating the mean sales over groups of three years (e.g. 2013–2014–2015, 2014–2015–2016, 2015–2016–2017) and plotting the results on a chart.

- Calculating a four-year moving average is more complex, making use of "centring" i.e. using a four-year and an eight-year moving total to establish a mid-point and further averages.

Variations are the difference between actual sales and the trend values.

Sales forecasting helps marketing planning and workforce planning, but it has several limitations, especially the fact that it ignores external factors, such as changes in consumer tastes and preferences, or competitors' marketing actions.

> **QUESTION PRACTICE**
>
> Define the term *four-part moving average*.   [2]

Response 1

A four-part moving average is a useful business tool for calculating average profit. It considers four years of financial data and calculates an average which can then be extrapolated to find a forecast for future years and identify trends. However Salaria believes this is not suitable.

This response could have achieved 1/2 marks.

Response 2

Four-part moving average.

A moving average is a statistical technique to get an overall idea of the trends in a data set. The aim is to smooth out short-term fluctuations and the trend is then measured by the moving averages.

If you have a period of x years (year 1 = t1, year 2 = t2, year 3 = t3 etc.), Y2 (the variable for t2) is calculated as $a_1 = (Y_1+Y_2+Y_3+Y_4)/4$, then for t3 it is $a_2 = (Y_2+Y_3+Y_4+Y_5)/4$, for t4 it is $a_3 = (Y_3+Y_4+Y_5+Y_6)/4$ etc. You can then centre the moving averages: for year 3 (t3), it is $(a_1+a_2)/2$, for year 4 (t4) it is $(a_2+a_3)/2$ etc.

This response could have achieved 2/2 marks.

▼ This definition is partial. The candidate has some good knowledge and understanding of "moving averages", but their definition does not refer to what is specific to a four-year moving average, as opposed to a three-year moving average. For a higher mark, the candidate should have mentioned "centring" (the calculation of averages over periods of four years in the time series, with trends mapped from year three onwards).

▲ This definition is clear and comprehensive; the candidate even explains how to calculate a moving average, which is beyond what was required here, but it confirms the fact that they understand the topic well.

>> **Assessment tip**

Although questions about moving averages are not frequent, make sure you know how to calculate three-year and four-year moving averages. It involves some simple arithmetic, adding and dividing; once you understand the principle, you will not have any difficulty.

Content link

Link to your IA

Even if your IA is not about marketing, you can apply the contents of this unit to your chosen organization. Do they have seasonal, cyclical or random variations? Do they use tools and techniques to forecast sales? If they do, can you assess the impact of forecast sales and variations from the trend on issues such as resources, costs and planning?

Content link

Link to other sub-units

Sub-units 4.3 and 1.5 are linked because the STEEPLE framework presented in 1.5 makes you consider the wide range of factors that may have an impact on sales, from predictable economic trends to unpredictable weather patterns.

Concept link

The concept of **change** is closely linked to the topic of sales forecasting, because sales forecasting is always affected by changes – some predictable, some not. For some small businesses, it can be a major problem, for example a baker needs to forecast as precisely as possible how many loaves of fresh bread they are going to sell the next day: if they bake too many, it will be a waste of resources, but if they bake too few, some customers will be disappointed.

4.4   MARKET RESEARCH

This sub-unit presents the forms, methods and sources of market research.

You should be able to:

✔ explain why and how organizations carry out market research

✔ distinguish between the different methods of primary market research

✔ distinguish between the different sources of secondary market research

✔ discuss ethical considerations of market research

✔ distinguish between qualitative and quantitative research

✔ distinguish between the different methods of sampling

✔ interpret results from data collection.

Topic summary

Market research is the process of collecting, analysing and reporting data related to a particular market. It has several purposes: it can help identify consumers' needs and wants, it can help measure customers' satisfaction and perception of a product, and it also enables organizations to make well-informed marketing decisions.

Market research can be carried out:

*   through **primary research** (also called "field research") to collect first-hand information, using the following methods: surveys (using questionnaires), interviews, focus groups, observations

*   through **secondary research** (also called "desk research") to use data that already exists, using the following sources: market analyses (market intelligence reports by special market research agents), academic journals (scholarly articles written by experts), government publications, media articles (in print or online).

▼ Table 4.4.1 The differences between **quantitative** and **qualitative** research

Quantitative research	Qualitative research
Collection of numerical data.	Collection of data about opinions, attitudes and beliefs.
Typical method: survey with closed questions.	Typical method: survey with open questions, interviews, focus groups.
Less open to interpretation.	High degree of interpretation.
Objective.	Subjective.
Concise and narrow focus.	Broad and complex focus.

Sampling is the process of selecting a group of people to represent the entire group of customers; this group is called "a sample of the population". The following six sampling techniques are used in marketing:

1. Quota sampling, with targets based on proportions.

2. Random sampling, with each person having an equal chance of being chosen.

3. Stratified sampling, creating strata (groups) of the whole population.

4. Cluster sampling, useful when the population is geographically dispersed.

5. Snowballing sampling, asking the first people sampled to recommend others (referrals).

6. Convenience sampling (also called "opportunity sampling") based on easy access and proximity to the researcher.

>> **Revision tip**

You must be able to explain the main advantages and disadvantages of all the six sampling methods. The following table outlines one advantage and one disadvantage of each:

Sampling method	One advantage	One disadvantage
Quota sampling	Findings are usually quite reliable because the sample is representative of all strata of the population.	The interviewer may be biased in the selection of who is interviewed.
Random sampling	Less bias, as everybody has an equal chance of being chosen.	May not be representative.
Stratified sampling	Very representative.	Not easy to do.
Cluster sampling	Quick method.	Potential for bias.
Snowballing sampling	Cost-effective and easy to do, through referrals.	Potential for bias.
Convenience sampling	Easy to do.	Potential for bias and not representative.

>> **Revision tip**

You must be able to explain the main advantages and disadvantages of all the methods and techniques of market research. The following tables outline one advantage and one disadvantage of each:

Primary market research

Method	One advantage	One disadvantage
Survey	Can collect large amount of data rapidly.	The respondents may not understand some of the questions and provide inaccurate answers.
Interview	Can achieve a high response rate.	Time consuming and costly.
Focus groups	Some participants may actively engage because of the interactions with others.	Some members may dominate or influence the group.
Observation	The market researcher can see how people behave in a given situation.	Should not be used alone as it only provides partial information.

Secondary market research

Method	One advantage	One disadvantage
Academic journal	Reliable because of the peer-review process.	So specialized that they may not always help for commercial market research.
Media articles	Easily available (in print and online).	May be too biased to help commercial market research.
Government publications	Usually trustworthy statistics and large-scale data about demographics.	May not be up to date.
Market analyses	Detailed and high-quality reports.	Usually expensive.

QUESTION PRACTICE

Secco Vineyards (SV) is a family-owned business producing wine in Sonoma, California. They mainly sell in local grocery stores where the competition is intense, so the manager has decided to conduct secondary market research about other possible markets in the US.

With reference to SV, explain **one** advantage **and one** disadvantage of using secondary market research.   [4]

SAMPLE STUDENT ANSWER

Response 1

▼ The candidate seemingly knows what "secondary market research" is, but the answer is too limited. The first sentence (about the advantage) seems to refer to "desk research" but the statement "doesn't have to do any physical work" is very vague, even if the examiner can guess that it means no collection of primary data. The second sentence shows some basic understanding of the disadvantages of secondary research (lack of accuracy, information not useful) however this is not applied to the case study.

> One advantage of secondary research is that SV doesn't have to do any physical work on their own. One disadvantage is that the research may not be very accurate, or it may not contain the information needed to make a business decision.

This response could have achieved 2/4 marks.

Response 2

▲ The advantage is clearly explained, with reference to the case study.

> One advantage of using secondary market research is that is very cost-effective. Secondary research is often free, and when it is not, it can be less expensive than the process of doing primary research. As SV is looking for other possible markets in the US, it would be very expensive and time-consuming to do research from Florida to Alaska and from Minnesota to Tennessee. For secondary research, Joe Secco only needs to read about wine consumption in different States.

One disadvantage of using secondary market research is that the information that Joe finds may not be directly useful and relevant for him – for example it may have been collected for a campaign to reduce alcohol consumption, so the conclusions may not be useful for him. Sources of secondary market research can be biased and subjective, so Joe must be careful as he wants to sell alcohol and this can be controversial.

▲ The disadvantage is clearly explained, with reference to the case study.

Note: The answer is clear, well-written and well-structured.

This response could have achieved 4/4 marks.

To know more about his customers, Jacob wanted to carry out primary research; he decided to use the method of convenience sampling.

Explain **one** advantage **and one** disadvantage for Jacob of using convenience sampling. [4]

>> **Assessment tip**

When it comes to market research, the terms "methods" and "techniques" are used interchangeably.

SAMPLE STUDENT ANSWER

An advantage is that the people he chooses in this convenience sampling method will be less likely to refuse to answer his questions than other people would. A disadvantage is that the results obtained from his research may be biased as his friends and relatives probably not only share backgrounds and opinions (we tend to be close with people who share our worldview), but would also probably share fewer negative opinions on MSS as they care about Jacob.

▼ The advantage is correct but not sufficiently applied; the candidate should have explained that convenience sampling means that Jacob knows the people he samples, which is why they are less likely to refuse to answer.

▲ The disadvantage is well explained and applied at the very end of the answer.

Note: 1 mark for the partial answer about the advantage. 2 marks for the good answer about the disadvantage.

This response could have achieved 3/4 marks.

 Content link

Link to your IA

Even if your IA is not about marketing, you can apply the contents of this sub-unit to your IA in two ways:

- How did you collect the data for your IA? Which methods of primary and/or secondary research did you use, and why? How did you analyse what you have collected?
- Does your chosen organization engage in market research? In which forms: using primary and/or secondary methods? How do they analyse the results?

 Content link

Link to other sub-units

Sub-units 4.4 and 4.1 are closely linked because a market orientation often involves market research in order to understand what customers need and want.

4.5   THE FOUR Ps (PRODUCT, PRICE, PROMOTION, PLACE)

This sub-unit focuses on the four Ps of the key model, the marketing mix of goods: product, price, promotion and place.

You should be able to:

- ✔ construct and explain the "product life cycle" model
- ✔ analyse:
  - ✔ the relationship between the product life cycle and the marketing mix
  - ✔ the relationship between the product life cycle, investment, profit and cash flow
- ✔ recommend extension strategies for a product
- ✔ apply the Boston Consulting Group (BCG) matrix to an organization's products and discuss its usefulness
- ✔ explain key aspects of branding: brand awareness, brand development, brand loyalty and brand value
- ✔ discuss the importance of branding
- ✔ discuss the importance of packaging
- ✔ evaluate the appropriateness of different pricing strategies
- ✔ distinguish between above the line promotion, below the line promotion and promotional mix
- ✔ discuss the impact of changing technology on promotional strategies
- ✔ discuss "guerrilla marketing" and its effectiveness as a promotional method
- ✔ explain the importance of place in the marketing mix
- ✔ evaluate the effectiveness of different types of distribution channels.

Topic summary

Product

The **product life cycle** model shows the five stages that a product goes through, from its introduction to the market:

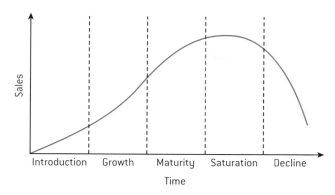

▲ **Figure 4.5.1** The product life cycle model

The product life cycle is closely linked to the marketing mix because different marketing actions will take place at different stages. For example, informative advertising will be particularly necessary in the introduction phase, and pricing strategies may change over time. The product life cycle is also linked to investment, profit and cash flow. For example, investing in promotion is needed in the introductory phase, when there is no profit and the cash flow is negative, whereas in the maturity phase investment is much lower, profit reaches its peak and the cash flow is positive.

Extension strategies are implemented at the maturity or saturation stages in order to avoid decline. Typical extension strategies include market development, new packaging or new promotional strategies.

Product portfolio analysis examines and compares the different products of a business. A tool commonly used for product portfolio analysis is the **Boston Consulting Group (BCG) matrix** that measures the relative market growth rate (low or high) and the relative market share (low or high) of the products of a company; they are then classified as "stars", "problem child", "cash cows" or "dogs":

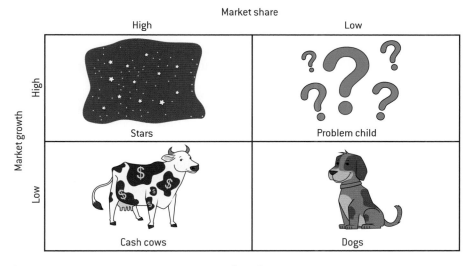

▲ **Figure 4.5.2** Boston Consulting Group (BCG) matrix

A **brand** is a name, symbol, sign or design that differentiates the products of one company from its competitors. Branding is very important because it has a strong influence on customer perception. The main aspects of branding are **brand awareness** (the ability of consumers to recognize the existence and availability of a company's product), **brand loyalty** (when consumers become committed to a brand and buy this brand repeatedly) and **brand value** (how much a brand is worth in terms of reputation and potential income).

Packaging plays several roles: it protects the product, it aids branding, it provides information in the contents and can add to the security (for example with anti-theft tabs).

Price

Price is the element of the marketing mix that generates revenue for the business.

The main pricing strategies are:

- **Cost-plus** pricing, easy to calculate by adding a mark-up to the cost of producing a product.

- **Penetration** pricing, with a low initial price to enter a market or launch a new product.

- **Skimming** pricing, with high prices at first to create a high value, high price image.

- **Psychological** pricing, with prices set to affect consumers' perception.

- **Loss leader** pricing, charging a low price for one product to attract consumers to buy other higher-priced ones.

- **Price discrimination** pricing, charging different prices to different groups of customers for the same product.

- **Competitive** pricing, charging according to competitors' prices.

- **Price leadership**, a form of competitive pricing to be the cheapest in the market.

- **Predatory** pricing, a form of competitive pricing to charge less than competitors in order to drive them out of the market.

Promotion

The aim of promotion is to obtain new customers or retain existing ones ("returning customers") by communicating information about the product. This can be done through:

- **above the line promotion**, paying for advertising in independent mass media such as television, radio or newspapers

- **below the line promotion**, through direct mail, trade shows, public relations and sales promotion; this is cheaper and more focused.

A successful **promotional mix** usually involves a balance of above the line and below the line promotional methods, coherently considering factors such as the cost, the target market and the type of product.

The impact of changing technology on promotional strategies can be seen in many ways, such as **viral marketing** (peer-to-peer communication to share messages rapidly and cheaply) as well as **social media marketing** and **social networking** (to build relationships and develop brand awareness and brand loyalty). **Guerrilla marketing** is a low-cost, flexible, unconventional marketing based on innovation and usually technology in order to create a "buzz".

Place

Place is about how the product reaches its customers, i.e. **distribution channels**, ranging from zero (direct: producer to consumer) to several (with intermediaries: agents, wholesalers, retailers).

>> **Assessment tip**

"Place" does not mean location in a geographical sense: it is about distribution. This is a common mistake made by students in their exam answers about the marketing mix.

>> **Assessment tip**

Make sure you know how to draw the BCG matrix, with the correct names in the correct places on the diagram (Stars, Problem child, Cash cows, Dogs). Do not forget the labels: "Market growth" and "Market share", "Low" and "High".

>> **Assessment tip**

Make sure you know how to draw the product life cycle model, with the correct names of the five stages in the correct places on the diagram. You also need to be able to relate the product life cycle to investment, profit and cash flow.

>> **Assessment tip**

There are often exam questions about the contents of this long unit, so make sure you revise it well. It is a very important one.

QUESTION PRACTICE

Utopia is a luxury holiday resort. It relies heavily on word of mouth for promotion and it has a very strong brand.

With reference to *Utopia*, explain two benefits of having a strong brand. [4]

SAMPLE STUDENT ANSWER

Examining Utopia's performance over time, it is without a doubt that they have achieved and effectively developed a strong brand. This refers to branding which is what differentiates Utopia from any other competitor in the market. In summary it is what makes a business unique and valuable for a target market. With Utopia achieving a strong brand, this would increase sales and profits in the long run, thus entailing an extended customer base, and therefore achieving customer loyalty. Also, obtaining a strong brand allows Utopia to make efficient use of their working capital to furthermore improve the brand in various aspects, along with coming up with new ideas such as the 3D printer to produce customized souvenirs in order to develop Utopia's offering of exceptional services to its customers; whether existing or potential.

▲ The answer starts with a definition of branding; this is not necessary and it does not result in any extra marks, but it shows that the candidate understands the topic of branding.

▲ The first benefit is well explained, linking an increase in sales and profit with brand loyalty.

▼ The second benefit links strong brand with working capital and investment, though it is less clear, especially in terms of continuously improving the brand: how is this a benefit? This could be better explained.

Note: The answer is clear overall, using the case study, though the second benefit could be better explained, for a higher score.

This response could have achieved 3/4 marks.

AFA is a business selling fair trade products (chocolate, coffee, clothing and stationery) in pop-up stalls and maybe online soon too.

With reference to *AFA*, explain the importance of branding. [6]

SAMPLE STUDENT ANSWER

▲ The candidate correctly uses terms about the importance of branding, such as "brand awareness".

▲ The occasional use of quotations from the case study helps ensure that the answer is not only theoretical, but linked to the case study.

▲ The candidate correctly uses business management in their answer, for example discussing "revenue stream" and "profit margins"; this shows that the candidate is not only knowledgeable about marketing, but about other parts of the subject too.

▲ The answer shows that the candidate knows about several roles and goals of branding.

▲ The candidate makes good links between different elements of the course, for example considering several stakeholders.

▲ The final part of the answer adds an original and less common idea about the importance of branding for one more stakeholder: employees. The candidate explains why some employees may be attracted to work for this company because of their brand and what it represents.

Branding is crucial to AFA as it helps to improve AFA's sales revenue through increased sales. It is important for AFA to develop a good brand image, to raise brand awareness so as to attract customers. Branding proved to be important to AFA, as their mission to supply fair trade products "were proving to be very popular with his customers". Customers recognized the mission of AFA and would help AFA to generate larger revenue stream and possibly profit margins with more sales.

Branding is also important at establishing the position in the market. Given that "AFA was a great success" and "sales revenue had grown significantly", it was likely that AFA had a large market share. This would be beneficial to AFA as it could give them advantages such as attracting suppliers and banks who would want to support AFA and gives AFA better bargaining power because of its strong brand presence. Thus, branding is important.

Branding is also important in attracting employees who share the same ideals and goals as AFA. AFA has branded itself as a business that is "fully dedicated to fair trade products", and Sam's focus on corporate social responsibility would brand the business in an ethical way, helping to attract employees who share the same vision as Sam. Thus, branding is important.

Note: This long answer is clear and well structured; it is particularly good to see how each paragraph presents an argument, with examples, and ends with "thus, branding is important". This helps ensure that the whole answer is focused and does not go off course, for example about other aspects of marketing.

This response could have achieved 6/6 marks.

Secco Vineyards (*SV*) is a family-owned business producing wine in Sonoma, California. Using cost-plus (mark-up) pricing, they sell their wine in local grocery stores. Competition is intense, so the managers are considering adopting other pricing strategies.

Given the intense competition, explain **two** pricing strategies *SV* might consider. [4]

SAMPLE STUDENT ANSWER

Response 1

Two pricing strategies that Secco Vineyards might consider could be odd-even pricing and mark-up pricing.

▼ Mark-up pricing is a pricing strategy that SV could consider, but the candidate does not explain why. The other answer (odd-even pricing) is not credited.

This response could have achieved 1/4 marks.

Response 2

The first pricing strategy they could use is loss leader: it means that they would sell one of their wines at a very low price (for example, one type of white wine) to attract new customers, and then they sell the other wines (for example, red wine) at a higher rate to make up for the loss on the while wine. This can help attract many new customers to SV wines.

▲ The first pricing strategy (loss leader) is suitable and well explained in context.

The second pricing strategy they could use is competitive pricing (predatory) given the "intense competition" (line 12) taking into account competitors' prices and charging just under.

▼ The second pricing strategy is relevant but it is not clearly explained; in particular, it is not clear how the company, having financial difficulties, could sustain a strategy of predatory pricing.

Note: The first pricing strategy is clear and well explained, the second less so.

This response could have achieved 3/4 marks.

QUESTION PRACTICE

Utopia is a luxury holiday resort. It relies heavily on word of mouth for promotion.

With reference to *Utopia*, explain the role of promotion.　　　　[6]

SAMPLE STUDENT ANSWER

Response 1

The promotion that Utopia currently uses is word of mouth for promotion. This is a kind of below the line promotion which does not use paid-for and mass media as the way to promote its products. Instead, word of mouth promotion relies on people spread out the information and inform other people about the product. Promotion is used to promote and sell its products and services to different existing or potential consumers. Since Utopia offers a unique and once in a lifetime tourist experience, their target consumers are relatively rich like the film stars. By using word of mouth, they may attract other film stars to experience their

▼ The candidate answers a different question about promotion, about word of mouth promotion – however this is not the question asked, even though there is the word "promotion".

▲ This sentence starts addressing the question: "promote and sell its products and services".

▼ The final part of the answer is not directly relevant: it is about word of mouth again, and viral marketing.

service. Plus, the viral marketing which spreads information through social network websites and email is a way for people knowing Utopia which reach its goal of promotion.

Note: The candidate wrote about forms of promotion, not about the role of promotion: to create awareness, to inform customers, to persuade them. Little in this short answer is relevant or can be credited.

This response could have achieved 2/6 marks.

Response 2

▲ The answer starts with a short definition, which is good practice.

Promotion is the act of advertising and giving information about a product to customers. The role of promotion at Utopia is extremely important.

▲ The candidate explains a first role of promotion (to attract new customers) with reference to the case study, as required.

First of all, promotion enables Utopia to attract more customers. Currently Utopia's promotion relies heavily on word of mouth. Although word of mouth is not a strong promotion strategy compared to above the line promotion strategies such as TV advertising, it will help Utopia attract new customers. By attracting more customers, Utopia will be able to generate more sales revenue.

▲ The candidate explains a second role of promotion (to build a positive brand image) again with reference to the case study, as required.

Moreover, promotion can also benefit Utopia by building a positive brand image. By promoting Utopia's exceptional once in a lifetime experience, Utopia will be able to build a positive brand image. A positive brand image is especially important for Utopia as it can lead to brand loyalty which would make customers make repeated purchases and this will give Utopia more profit.

Note: The answer is good overall, though it could be more developed, for an even higher mark. Everything written is correct, and the structure is clear, but the examiner would expect a longer answer with other points about the role of promotion.

This response could have achieved 5/6 marks.

🔗 Content link
Link to other sub-units

- Sub-units 4.5 and 4.2 are closely linked because 4.2 introduces the marketing mix in the wider context of marketing planning.
- Sub-units 4.5 and 4.6 are closely linked because the extended marketing mix of services (seven Ps) builds on the marketing mix of goods (four Ps).

🔗 Content link
Link to your IA

Even if your IA is not about marketing, you can use and apply the contents of this chapter to your chosen organization. You could prepare a four Ps analysis of one of their products, you could examine their promotional mix or their distribution channel, or you could also study their pricing strategy.

Concept link

The concepts of **innovation** and **strategy** are linked to the topic of the four Ps:

- **Innovation** is required in all aspects of the marketing mix, from product development to packaging (e.g. reducing unnecessary use of plastic wrapping) to promotion (e.g. creative use of new technologies such as viral marketing on social media).

- **Strategy**, because the four Ps are interrelated within a coherent marketing strategy. Changes in one "P" have an impact on the others, for example starting to sell online and distribute through e-commerce may require changes in the promotion channels, or launching a new product may involve a skimming strategy for that specific product, which requires clear communication to manage the brand well.

4.6 THE EXTENDED MARKETING MIX OF SEVEN Ps (HL ONLY)

You should be able to:

✔ explain the meaning of the seven Ps model in a service-based market

✔ discuss the importance:

✔ of employee-customer relationships in marketing a service

✔ of delivery processes in marketing a service

✔ of tangible physical evidence in marketing a service.

This sub-unit focuses on the three Ps of the extended marketing mix of services: people, processes and physical evidence.

Topic summary

The **seven Ps model** is composed of the four Ps of the marking mix of goods, plus three Ps specific to the **marketing of services**. Due to the intangible nature of services, other aspects of marketing are important:

- **People** refers to the employees, especially the customer-fronting ones who are the face of the organization, for example the receptionist of a hotel.

- **Process** refers to the procedures and policies to ensure access to the service, for example the online system for a hotel reservation.

- **Physical evidence** refers to the appearance and visible aspects that the customer will encounter, for example the cleanliness and style of the lobby and bedroom of the hotel.

Revision tip

Services require an extended marketing mix (three extra Ps) because other elements are important for customers. The marketing of services is therefore more complex than the marketing of goods.

Marketing of goods	Marketing of services
Product, price, place, promotion	Product, price, place, promotion
	+ People, processes, physical evidence

Although there are not often questions about the extended marketing mix, you must know and understand the three extra Ps and their relevance for services, as opposed to physical tangible goods.

 Content link

Link to your IA

Even if your IA is not about marketing, you can use and apply the contents of this sub-unit to your chosen organization. To what extent is the extended marketing mix of the seven Ps relevant to it? Can you apply the three extra Ps to some of their work?

 Content link

Link to other sub-units

Sub-units 4.5 and 4.6 are closely linked because the extended marketing mix of services (seven Ps) builds on the marketing mix of goods (four Ps).

Concept link

The concepts of **culture** and **innovation** are linked to the topic of the extended marketing mix:

- **Cultural** differences may lead to variations in service delivery, as employees' attitudes, beliefs and values may be different; this can cause misunderstanding or even conflict, for example when tourists do not receive the same level of service as in their own countries.

- **Innovation** is required in all aspects of the extended marketing mix: processes (e.g. online booking/purchasing), people (e.g. availability of customer service in different languages) and physical evidence (e.g. creativity and originality in architecture and interior design).

4.7 INTERNATIONAL MARKETING (HL ONLY)

You should be able to:

✔ analyse the main methods of entry into international markets

✔ discuss the opportunities and threats posed by entry into international markets

✔ discuss the strategic and operational implications of international marketing

✔ examine the role of cultural differences in international marketing

✔ examine the implications of globalization on international marketing.

This sub-unit focuses on the marketing of goods and services across national boundaries.

Topic summary

Global marketing refers to companies that have a standardized approach to market their products in the same way in all countries, whereas **international marketing** implies that companies adapt their marketing to suit the culture and different expectations of their customers in different countries.

The main methods of entry into international markets are:

- **E-commerce**: trading over the internet.

- **Exporting**: directly or indirectly, through an agent or by "piggybacking".

- **Foreign direct investment**: setting a production plant (factory) in another country.

- **International joint venture**: setting up a new company in partnership with a local one.

- **International franchising**: granting a franchise to a franchisee in another country.

Entry into international markets provides many opportunities, such as market development, enhanced brand image and economies of scale. It also poses many threats, especially socio-cultural challenges, legal challenges and economic challenges.

>> **Assessment tip**

There are not often questions specifically about international marketing, but you must know and understand the topic, as you may refer to it in your answers to other questions, for example about external growth or market development.

Content link
Link to other sub-units

- Sub-units 4.7 and 1.5 are linked because the STEEPLE framework presented in 1.5 may help examine the threats and opportunities arising from international commerce.

- Sub-units 4.7 and 1.6 are linked because 1.6 explains joint ventures and franchising, two methods of entry into international markets.

- Sub-units 4.7 and 4.8 are linked because 4.8 explains e-commerce, another method of entry into international markets.

Content link
Link to your IA

Even if your IA is not about marketing, you can use and apply the contents of this sub-unit to your chosen organization. Do they engage in international marketing? If yes, what opportunities and threats have they encountered?

All six concepts help understand the topic of international marketing:

- **Ethics**, because international marketing means trading across national borders, with customers who may have different ethical values, beliefs and attitudes (so for example some promotional material may need to be revised, as it may be unacceptable in the other country).

- **Culture**, because the company may need to employ a local workforce who may have different views about leadership, management and motivation (so HR practices that work well in one country, for example flexitime, performance-related pay or cellular manufacturing may not be appropriate in another one).

- **Change**, because entry into foreign markets implies many changes in the organization, in all areas, from finance (payment in foreign currencies) to logistics (to ensure distribution in other countries, possibly other continents) and from HR (with the need for translators) to legal affairs (to ensure compliance with national standards and regulations).

- **Globalization**, because international marketing is at the core of the phenomenon of globalization. A cornerstone of globalization is the way goods and services spread around the world, so globalization depends on international marketing, especially in terms of trade and distribution.

- **Innovation**, because some products may need to be modified and adapted for the international market, to suit customers themselves (for example their taste in food), their culture (for example cars with the steering wheel on the right or left side) or to conform to the country's legislation (for example health and safety).

- **Strategy**, because going into foreign markets is a strategic decision requiring much planning in all business functions (not only marketing but also operations, HR and finance) in order to achieve long-term goals (corresponding to international market development in the Ansoff matrix).

4.8   E-COMMERCE

This sub-unit focuses on e-commerce, the buying and selling of goods and services via the internet.

You should be able to:

✔ describe the main features of e-commerce

✔ explain the effects of changing technology and e-commerce on the marketing mix

✔ distinguish between the main categories of e-commerce

✔ discuss the costs and benefits of e-commerce to businesses and consumers.

Topic summary

The main features of **e-commerce** are its availability, the fact that it is present almost everywhere in the world (with some exceptions), the possibilities for customization (as users may personalize it and adapt it to their needs and context), and the possibility to integrate text and images with audio and video.

Due to technological progress and innovation over the last twenty years, e-commerce has had an impact on all aspects of the marketing mix, especially place (distribution), promotion (online advertising with the option to purchase straightaway) and process (both the online purchase and the logistics of delivery).

The three main categories of e-commerce are:

- **Business to business (B2B).**
- **Business to consumer (B2C).**
- **Consumer to consumer (C2C).**

Benefits of e-commerce include a wider market reach (market development), cost effectiveness and convenience. The costs of e-commerce are internet security concerns (with online payment), increased competition (with worldwide competitors), dependency on a reliable and stable internet connection and possible information overload.

> **》 Revision tip**
>
> Make sure that you can explain the main differences between B2B, B2C and C2C from the perspective of the seller and also from the perspective of the buyer. You may be familiar with e-commerce from a customer's perspective, purchasing online from a company (B2C) or from another person (C2C). The B2C model is the most popular one, but C2C platforms are developing fast. The two are sometimes blurred as some businesses can also sell on C2C platforms, such as eBay and Airbnb. The third category of e-commerce (B2B) is about businesses buying products from each other, for example wholesalers and retailers.

> **》 Assessment tip**
>
> If you have an exam question about e-commerce, remember that you must answer it in an academic way, with marketing terminology, and not only with generic, common sense ideas based on your experience as a consumer.

QUESTION PRACTICE

AFA is a business selling fair trade products (chocolate, coffee, clothing and stationery) in pop-up stalls and maybe online soon too.

With reference to *AFA*, outline **one** benefit and **one** cost to Sam of opening a new e-commerce website. [4]

SAMPLE STUDENT ANSWER

Response 1

One benefit for Sam about opening an e-commerce is that in this way he is following his vision statement or improving the lines of internal and external stakeholders and creating benefits for them as the e-commerce would be beneficial for consumers and for employers. One cost to Sam is that by opening an e-commerce, competition may arise as their products and prices could be copied or used by competition in order to make a competition pricing strategy and decreasing sales for AFA that could make Sam take decisions against his vision statement.

▼ The answer about the benefit is not clear: the candidate only states that there are benefits for consumers and employees – but what are the benefits?

▼ The cost is not clear: products and prices being copied by competitors? It is not clear what the candidate means.

Note: Although the candidate knows what e-commerce means, and uses business terminology in their answer ("stakeholders", "vision statement"), the candidate does not clearly answer the question about one cost and one benefit.

This response could have achieved 0/4 marks.

Response 2

▲ The benefit is clearly outlined, in context, with business terminology ("channels of distribution", "diseconomies of scale").

Opening a new e-commerce site allows AFA to exploit more channels of distribution, and reach out to a wider international market. This is in line with Sam's eventual goal to "operate at a global level". It also complements the "brick and mortar retail outlets", as it provides greater convenience to the customer, and reduces rental costs. This is important to AFA, as it is already experiencing increased costs from diseconomies of scale. E-commerce allows AFA to grow to a possibly global scale, without the rental expenses of growth by opening physical stores.

▲ The cost is clearly outlined, in context, with business terminology ("overheads", "supply chain").

That said, an e-commerce site also introduces greater logistical complexity, and may lead to greater stock-holding costs, or administrative overheads. This would further add to the diseconomies of scale and coordination issues experienced at AFA. Having three difference avenues from which products are sold (stall, store, e-commerce), greatly complicates management and supply chain logistics.

Note: The answer is clear, thorough and well-written.

This response could have achieved 4/4 marks.

 Content link

Link to your IA

Even if your IA is not specifically about marketing, you can use and apply the contents of this sub-unit to your chosen organization. Do they engage in e-commerce? In B2B or B2C? How has it altered their marketing mix? Did they encounter particular challenges?

 Concept link

The concepts of innovation and globalization are closely linked to e-commerce:

- **Innovation**, because the rise of the internet and the development of related technologies (such as online payment) have facilitated the development of e-commerce for both goods and services.

- **Globalization**, because e-commerce has been a key catalyst of globalization. E-commerce means that increasing volumes of goods, services and financial payments cross national boundaries.

Content link

Link to other sub-units

- Sub-units 4.8 and 4.5/4.6 are linked because e-commerce impacts on several aspects of the marketing mix, especially place, promotion and processes.

- Sub-units 4.8 and 4.7 are linked because e-commerce has two dimensions: national (domestic) and international; the latter raises issues of import taxes and differences in legal standards.

5 OPERATIONS MANAGEMENT

You should know:

✔ The role of operations management

✔ Production methods

✔ Lean production and quality management (HL only)

✔ Location

✔ Production planning (HL only)

✔ Research and development (HL only)

✔ Crisis management and contingency planning (HL only)

5.1 THE ROLE OF OPERATIONS MANAGEMENT

You should be able to:

✔ define operations management and outline its relationship to other business functions

✔ analyse operations management in organizations producing goods and/or services

✔ recommend operations management strategies and practices for ecological, social and economic sustainability.

This sub-unit introduces the business function that deals with the production of goods and services: operations management.

Topic summary

Operations are the fundamental activities of all organizations. The term can be defined as "what they do and deliver"; another word for it is "production". The three other business functions support and enable operations:

• Human resources – because operations are done by people.

• Accounts and finance – because operations need to be funded.

• Marketing – because operations produce goods and services that must be promoted, marketed and sold in order to generate revenue.

Operations management is influenced by economic, social and environmental factors. Operations should aim to be **sustainable** in those three areas. This model is called "triple bottom line", with three words starting with the letter P: Profit, People and Planet. The topic of sustainability is becoming increasingly important in business management: decisions such as growth and expansion should consider not only financial impacts, but also human impacts and environmental impacts.

Content link

Link to your IA

Even if your IA is not about operations management, you can apply the contents of this sub-unit to your chosen organization. What are its key operations? What goods and services are produced – and by whom? What role does operations management play in the organization? The organization you chose for your IA gives you the chance to learn more about the contents of this sub-unit in context.

Test yourself

Explain why each P of the "triple bottom line" model of sustainability is important but also difficult to achieve.

>> Assessment tip

There are not often questions about operations management in broad terms, but for the paper 1 case study and for the paper 2 stimulus materials, it is important:

- that you identify the organization's key operations
- that you identify how these operations are linked to the other business functions of the organization.

This will help you to understand the purpose of the organization and recommend possible strategies, for example to increase workforce capabilities, to modify the goods and services produced, or to invest in more equipment.

Content link

Link to other sub-units

- Sub-unit 1.1 about entrepreneurship and business start-up is linked to this sub-unit because a business plan must describe the operations (i.e. what the organization will physically do).
- Sub-unit 2.1 about workforce planning and recruitment is linked to this sub-unit because the workforce size depends on the level of operations.
- Sub-unit 3.8 about investment appraisal is linked to this sub-unit because investment usually enables an improvement or an increase in operations.
- Sub-unit 4.5 about the product part of the marketing mix, because products are created by operations.

Concept link

All six concepts are linked to the topic of operations:

- **Ethics,** because sustainability has a strong ethical foundation: sustainable organizations are the ones that behave ethically and understand their impact on people and on the natural environment, rather than just considering finance and profit.
- **Culture,** because sustainable development implies respecting local workers' traditions, values and customs.
- **Globalization,** because even small companies can operate globally, for example importing or exporting goods.
- **Change,** because all companies change their operations over time, adapting to customers' demands or to other external factors, from competitors or new legislation.
- **Strategy,** because organizations' strategic decisions always have an impact on their operations, for example regarding developing new products or diversifying.
- **Innovation,** because all innovations in processes or in products are meant to make operations more efficient.

5.2 PRODUCTION METHODS

You should be able to:

This sub-unit introduces the main methods of production of goods.

✔ distinguish between the following methods of production:

   ✔ job production (also called "customized production")

   ✔ batch production

   ✔ mass production

✔ explain the principles of "flow production" and "cellular manufacturing"

✔ recommend the most appropriate method of production for a given situation.

Topic summary

There are three methods of production:

- **Job production** (also called "customized production") is market-oriented: customers decide what the product should be, for example a personalized birthday cake with your name in it.

- **Batch production** is a group of identical products, made in groups ("batches"), for example a dozen cakes with the same flavour.

- **Mass production** (also called "flow production" and "process production") creates a high volume of standardized products (for example identical loaves of bread).

They each have advantages and disadvantages. Mass production, for example, can achieve economies of scale, unlike job production; however, it is a based on the principle of "product orientation" which, in marketing terms, is not always suitable as it is not market-led.

The terms **flow production**, **line production** and **process production** refer to specific aspects of mass production in factories using a continuous flow of materials and producing goods in stages.

The term **cellular manufacturing** (also called "cell production") refers to a form of manufacturing where teams of workers are responsible for certain parts of the production. Cellular manufacturing could apply to all methods of production; however batch production is the most common one.

In each situation, one method may be more appropriate than others, depending on several factors, such as the target market, the state of technology and the availability of resources, as well as government regulations.

Test yourself

Can you represent each method of production in the form of a diagram or a flow chart? This is not an exam question, but this creative challenge can help you check that you understand the differences between job production, batch production and mass production.

This question refers to a company called *AS* that uses cellular manufacturing.

Describe **two** advantages for *AS* of using cellular manufacturing in the production of its solar power systems.   [4]

Response 1

▼ The first bullet point is a definition rather than the description of an advantage.

▲ The second bullet point (reduction of cost, time and hassle) is a correct advantage, with some application to the case study (explicit reference to the solar power systems).

- Cellular manufacturing is a process of producing parts of a product in different cells located next to each other.
- Using cellular manufacturing reduces the cost and time consumed for production. Splitting the work between cells will reduce the issue of transportation and each team can focus on their assigned work at the same time. This reduces hassle between divisions and can produce more solar power systems in such a less time.

Note: The candidate knows about cellular manufacturing, which is what the question aims to assess.

For a higher mark, the candidate should have written about a second advantage, such as an increase in workers' motivation through job enlargement.

This response could have achieved 2/4 marks.

Response 2

▲ Although the candidate does not use the word "advantages", the examiner recognizes that the two points made are advantages (increase in employee motivation and production of higher quality goods).

Cellular manufacturing can lead to more employee motivation, as employees work together as a team and build relationships with other workers.

Cellular manufacturing can produce higher quality goods as production is split into sections, and workers in each section would be specialized and efficient.

Note: The response is good but too theoretical: there is no reference to the context of the case study; this is necessary for top marks in business management exam answers.

This response could have achieved 2/4 marks.

🔗 Content link

Link to your IA

Even if your IA is not about operations management, you could apply the contents of this sub-unit to your chosen organization if they manufacture goods. What method(s) of production do they use, and why? What are the advantages and the disadvantages?

➤➤ Assessment tip

Command terms are very important: you can always get some points if you show your knowledge of the course contents, but for full marks your answer must do what you what are asked to do in the question. To assess that you know the meaning of "cellular manufacturing", the exam question could be:

1) "Define cellular manufacturing." [2 marks]

Or

2) "Describe an advantage of cellular manufacturing." [2 marks]

Example 1

A candidate writes the following:

"Cellular manufacturing is a form of manufacturing where workers are motivated and work in teams called 'cells'. The flow production line is composed of these cells that are self-contained units each responsible for a part of the finished product."

As an answer to question 1), this would score 2 marks, as it is a clear definition. As an answer to Question 2) however, it would only score 1 mark because the advantage (greater worker motivation) is too briefly outlined, and not described. The candidate shows some knowledge of cellular manufacturing and the examiner rewards this, but the candidate cannot score maximum marks as they did not properly answer the question asked, with the command term "describe".

Example 2

A candidate writes the following:

"Cellular manufacturing workers are more motivated because they work in teams, communicate a lot more between colleagues and do a range of jobs and tasks inside the cell."

This answer describes an advantage of cellular manufacturing. As an answer to Question 2), it would score 2 marks. As an answer to Question 1), it would only score 1 mark because the candidate shows some knowledge but only writes a partial definition and does not properly answer the question asked.

Content link

Link to other sub-units

- Sub-unit 2.2 about organizational structure is linked to this sub-unit.

- Sub-unit 2.4 about motivation is linked to this sub-unit.

Concept link

All concepts are linked to the topic of production methods, especially change and innovation:

- **Change**, because the choice of production methods will change over time, for example if the organization starts to offer highly specialized, one-off products that require job production.

- **Innovation**, because process innovation may result in more efficient techniques: this is how fast food restaurants developed in the twentieth century.

5.3 LEAN PRODUCTION AND QUALITY MANAGEMENT (HL ONLY)

You should be able to:

✔ define lean production and describe its main features

✔ distinguish between the following methods of lean production:

    ✔ continuous improvement (*kaizen*)

    ✔ just-in-time (JIT)

    ✔ *kanban*

    ✔ *andon*

✔ explain the features of "cradle to cradle" design and manufacturing

✔ distinguish between quality control and quality assurance

This sub-unit examines the features and methods of lean production and the principles of quality management.

✔ explain the following methods of managing quality:

  ✔ quality circle

  ✔ benchmarking

  ✔ total quality management (TQM)

✔ evaluate the impact of lean production and TQM on an organization

✔ discuss the importance of national and international quality standards.

Topic summary

Operations management is increasingly using principles of **lean management** in order to cut waste, be more efficient, save money and be more sustainable.

Lean management uses several methods such as:

- *Kaizen*, a Japanese term that refers to continuous improvement and continuous changes at all levels of the organization in order to improve processes.

- **Just-in-time** (JIT) to reduce the stocks of both raw materials and finished products.

- *Kanban*, an IT system supporting JIT to ensure a steady flow of production without any waste, for example with barcodes and smooth communication throughout the organization.

- *Andon*, an automatic signalling system informing workers and managers when there is a problem in production, because of quality, process or product.

Cradle to cradle (C2C) design and manufacturing is a new model of sustainability stating that once a product is used, it should be recycled in order to recreate the same product.

Quality control and quality assurance should ensure that all products are safe, reliable and offer value for money. **Quality control** means inspecting finished products to check that they meet the desired level of quality, whereas **quality assurance** monitors quality standards across the entire production process.

Managing quality can be done in several ways, such as:

- **Quality circles**: groups of volunteers who meet to discuss ways of improving quality.

- **Benchmarking**: comparing products against competitors' products.

- **Total quality management (TQM)**: an approach to improving quality across the organization, combining several quality tools such as quality chains (involving suppliers) and SPC (Statistical Process Control) data.

Lean production and TQM are closely linked; they have many advantages, such as the fact that they can reduce costs (especially in the long term), but also disadvantages, such as the fact that it may take time to change the culture and practices of an organization.

National and international quality standards are increasingly important in all industries. Meeting recognized standards can help businesses that want to export, giving a competitive edge and reassuring potential customers.

Describe **one** method of lean production **other than** recycling.   [2]

SAMPLE STUDENT ANSWER

> With lean production being the process of reducing waste to boost overall efficiency and performance of a certain organization, JIT would be a highly appropriate method of lean production. JIT is a stock control system where the business would keep zero or minimum stock in order to improve the efficiency of the working capital, along with the efficiency of stocks themselves. There will be less storage costs, yet Utopia may run out of stock in the case of an unexpected order (demand).

▲ The method of lean production chosen by the candidate is JIT. There were several other possible responses such as *kanban*, *kaizen*, *andon* etc.

Note: The description of JIT is clear and shows full understanding.

This response could have achieved 2/2 marks.

>> **Assessment tip**

Make sure you know precise definitions of all the terms in this sub-unit – as there are often exam questions asking you to define *kaizen*, *andon* or TQM.

Test yourself

Explain the difference between quality control and quality assurance.

Content link

Link to other sub-units

- Sub-unit 5.1 where the topic of sustainability is introduced, with the definition of "triple bottom line": lean management is a strategy to make an organization more sustainable.

- Sub-unit 5.5 where JIT is further explained with the comparison of two methods: JIT (just-in-time) and JIC (just-in-case).

Content link

Link to your IA

Even if your IA is not about operations management, you could apply the contents of this sub-unit to your chosen organization. Do they use principles of lean management, benchmarking or TQM? How do they control the quality of the goods they produce?

Concept link

All concepts are linked to the topic of production methods, especially **globalization** and **change**, as well as **culture** and **innovation**:

- **Globalization** and **change**, because the increasing number of international quality standards (in all industries, from manufacturing toys and pharmaceutical drugs to hospitality) contributes to the phenomenon of globalization, leading to changes in operations throughout the world.

- **Innovation** and **culture**, because the modern methods of lean production (such as *kaizen* and *andon*) were first developed in South East Asia in the second half of the twentieth century, before spreading to the rest of the world.

5.4 LOCATION

This sub-unit focuses on the reasons for the choice of a specific location for a production facility, and on the factors to consider when relocating a business.

You should be able to:

✔ analyse the reasons for the choice of location of production

✔ evaluate the following ways of relocating production, either nationally or internationally:

  ✔ outsourcing/subcontracting

  ✔ offshoring

  ✔ insourcing.

Topic summary

One of the most important decisions that a business has to make is where it will locate (or relocate) production. Numerous factors influence the **choice of the location** or **relocation** of a production facility, such as cost (of land, labour and transport), competition, available infrastructure and transport/logistics networks, land, labour pool (human resources nearby), government (and local authorities), proximity to suppliers, familiarity with the area etc.

Outsourcing (subcontracting) is the practice of using another business (as a "third party") to complete some parts of the work ("peripheral activities"); the organization can then focus on its core activity. **Offshoring** is an extension of outsourcing: it means outsourcing to another country ("offshore" = overseas, abroad). **Insourcing** (in-housing) is the opposite: it is the practice of performing peripheral activities internally, for example to be able to control costs or quality. **Reshoring** is the process of bringing these activities back into the home country.

QUESTION PRACTICE

This question is about Su, the owner of a business called *Afghan Sun*. For the location of the plant, Su hesitates between two very different locations, in two countries called A and B.

Su is considering two possible locations for the production facility. Explain the factors (reasons) that Su may consider when deciding between the two locations. [6]

SAMPLE STUDENT ANSWER

Response 1

Location refers to the geographic site of a business.

A factor that Su may consider when deciding between the two is the government assistance that the locations offer. Since Su needs some more financial assistance for Afghan Sun, this may be a very important factor for her to consider. Su may lean

▲ The first sentence (definition of location) is not necessary but it enables the candidate to focus their mind on the topic of the question and to show the examiner that they know the meaning of "location" in this context.

more towards location B as location B encourages investments from overseas with grants available. This description fits Afghan Sun perfectly, and through this Su may be able to reduce the cost of production of her main facility further in order to enable a very low price to be charged (line 24). Therefore, Su and her production team may want to consider this external factor to decide between the two locations.

Another factor that Su may consider when deciding between the two locations is the facilities of the two locations. The facilities are important because it will act as the fixed cost of the whole production, no matter how much solar power Su's factory produces, it will not change. Thus it's best to choose a facility with lower rent to keep her costs of production low. For location A, the facilities require new facilities and high rent, Su may not be able to cover the costs of it as she doesn't have a great lot of funds at the moment (250K from table 2).

▲ The first factor (availability of government assistance) is well explained, with reference to the case study. The candidate does not only explain why government assistance is important for Su's company, but also why it can be a factor to help choose between the two countries (location B rather than location A).

▲ The second factor (facilities) is well explained, with reference to the case study. The candidate does not only explain why this factor is important for Su, but also why location A is not suitable, as it would be too expensive regarding facilities (with the need to construct new ones and to pay high rent for them).

Note: The answer is good and clearly structured. The candidate duly explains two factors that both lead to the selection of country B for the location of the production facility.

The question refers to "factors" in the plural; two was the minimum number, which is what the candidate has given.

The candidate integrates elements from the case study well in the answer, for example about the financial resources available ($250K, see last sentence).

The candidate could have added a conclusion at the end to recap the points made and to state that other factors could/should also be taken into consideration, such as political stability or infrastructure.

This response could have achieved 5/6 marks.

Content link
Link to your IA

Even if your IA is not about operations management, you could apply the contents of this sub-unit to your chosen organization. Where are they located? Why? What factors made them choose this location? What would be the advantages and disadvantages of a relocation?

Content link
Link to other sub-units

- Sub-unit 1.6 about growth includes several points about location and relocation, such as the role and impact of globalization or the reasons for the growth of multinational companies.
- Sub-unit 2.1 about workforce planning introduces the topics of outsourcing and offshoring.
- Sub-unit 2.2 about organizational structure presents different models (such as organization by region or Handy's "Shamrock") that may be suitable when location is relocated or outsourced.

Concept link

All concepts are linked to the topics of location and relocation:

- **Globalization** has an impact on location, with both "pull factors" (encouraging companies to locate abroad) and "push factors" (attracting companies to a particular place) for example with tax incentives.

- Relocating is a major **strategic** decision that senior managers never take lightly, as it involves numerous **changes**, not only in terms of geography, but also in terms of legislation, language and **culture** (as it may be in a country with different laws, language, values and habits).

- Relocating will also affect both the structure and the **culture** of the organization, as it will imply substantial **changes** in the workforce, with new employees arriving.

- **Ethical** aspects must be considered too, as employees may not be able and willing to move to another town or even another country, if their employer relocates.

- The ecosystem and culture of **innovation** in a particular city or region may be a factor that leads new start-ups to locate there, for example Bengaluru in India or Silicon Valley in the USA.

5.5   PRODUCTION PLANNING (HL ONLY)

This sub-unit focuses on the process of planning production, organizing supply chains, implementing methods of stock control and calculating production ratios.

You should be able to:

✔ explain the supply chain process

✔ distinguish between just-in-case (JIC) and just-in-time (JIT)

✔ construct and interpret stock control charts based on lead time, buffer stock, re-order level and re-order quantity

✔ calculate and interpret:

    ✔ capacity utilization rate

    ✔ productivity rate

    ✔ cost to buy (CTB)

    ✔ cost to make (CTM).

Topic summary

The **supply chain** is the system of connected organizations that allow a business to fulfil its activities and reach its customers. It includes several external stakeholders: the suppliers, distributors and retailers.

The two **methods of stock control** are:

- **Just-in-case (JIC):** a traditional method where stock levels of raw materials and of finished products are high, in case of a sudden increase in demand.

- **Just-in-time (JIT):** a more modern method where raw materials are supplied only when necessary, and where goods are produced only when there is an order, without stock of finished products.

JIC and JIT both have advantages and disadvantages – for example JIC may reduce costs by buying in bulk and thus getting discounts from suppliers, but JIT does not require storage space.

Holding stock can be expensive; several elements must be taken into consideration when deciding on stock control, especially:

- Maximum stock level.

- Minimum stock level (also called "**buffer stock**").

- **Lead time** (between ordering new stock of raw materials and receiving it).

- Optimal stock level.

- Re-order level and re-order quantity.

- Nature of stock (may be perishable).

In order to know how efficient a facility is, production managers can calculate its **capacity utilization rate**:

$$\text{Capacity utilization rate} = \frac{\text{Actual output}}{\text{Maximum productive capacity}} \times 100$$

To measure the efficiency of production, managers can also calculate the **productivity rate**:

$$\text{Productivity rate} = \frac{\text{Total output}}{\text{Total input}} \times 100$$

One business decision is whether to buy or to make: it may sometimes be cheaper for a business to buy a product made elsewhere, and even to import it, rather than manufacture it.

- **CTB (cost to buy)** is calculated by multiplying Price by Quantity.

- **CTM (cost to make)** is calculated by multiplying Variable Costs by Quantity, and adding Fixed Costs.

$$\text{CTB} = \text{P} \times \text{Q}$$

$$\text{CTM} = (\text{CV} \times \text{Q}) + \text{FC}$$

> **>> Assessment tip**
>
> If you have to calculate a ratio (such as capacity utilization rate or productivity rate), do not forget to include the percentage sign in your answer. Even if the calculation is correct, without the % sign you would not achieve the maximum mark.

> **>> Revision tip**
>
> As you revise this sub-unit, you should identify some companies you know that use JIC and some others that use JIT, and explain why: does it depend on the sector, on the type and size of business, on its culture, on its marketing or finance? These examples will help you consolidate your knowledge of the differences between JIT and JIC.

> **Content link**
> **Link to other sub-units**
>
> - Sub-unit 4.5 about the P for Place of the marketing mix refers to the effectiveness of different types of distribution channels, according to the number of intermediaries.
>
> - Sub-unit 5.3 about lean management refers to the topic of JIT as JIT is one of the methods enabling companies to be "lean" and more efficient.

> **Content link**
> **Link to your IA**
>
> Even if your IA is not about operations management, you could apply the contents of this sub-unit to your chosen organization. How would you describe their supply chain? How do they control their stock? Can you calculate their capacity utilization rate and their productivity rate?

The concepts of **change**, **strategy** and **innovation** are linked to the topic of production planning:

- **Change** because calculating production ratios (and comparing trends) may help managers understand what may need to be changed to improve productivity (for example: tighter control of the resource input from suppliers).

- **Strategy** because decisions about methods of stock control may be strategic (and not just operational), as they may require consideration of long-term implications as part of a company-wide strategic plan.

- **Innovation** because the supply chain may always be subject to innovation and improvement: JIT itself was innovative when it was first developed in Japan in the 1960s and 1970s.

5.6   RESEARCH AND DEVELOPMENT (HL ONLY)

This sub-unit focuses on the importance of R&D (research and development) in all organizations, no matter how big or small they are.

You should be able to:

✔ discuss the importance of research and development for a business

✔ explain the importance of developing goods and services that address customers' unmet needs

✔ distinguish between four types of innovation

✔ discuss how pace of change in an industry, organizational culture and ethical considerations may influence R&D practices and strategies in an organization

✔ explain the difference between *adaptive creativity* (adapting something that exists) and *innovative creativity* (creating something new).

Topic summary

Research and development (R&D) is important in all industries. Large businesses often have departments specifically called "R&D", but innovation occurs in all sectors and in all organizations: even a small local bakery can be innovative, offering new cakes and new types of bread. R&D is not just about design technology: all companies engage in R&D in their own way.

Innovation can take different forms:

- **Product innovation** refers to the creation of entirely new products, or the development of existing ones (as extension strategies in a product life cycle).

- **Process innovation** refers to improving the manufacturing or service delivery process (for example JIT was a process innovation).

- **Positioning innovation** refers to the use or perception of a new product; in terms of marketing, it is more about promotion than about the product itself.

- **Paradigm innovation** refers to a radical innovation that can change a whole industry, for example the development of budget airlines, of online banking and of e-commerce.

The aim is to develop goods and services that address customers' unmet needs. Successful R&D has many advantages for a business, such as enhancing the image of the company and motivating the workforce; there are disadvantages too, such as opportunity costs as investing in R&D means not investing in other areas such as promotion.

Creativity is an essential part of R&D. *Adaptive creativity* transfers and applies existing forms of thinking and problem-solving to new scenarios, whereas *innovative creativity* generates new forms of thinking, addressing problems from a new perspective.

Numerous factors may influence R&D in an organization, such as organizational culture, technology and past experience.

>> Assessment tip

This sub-unit is based on the concept of innovation, one of the six concepts in the syllabus, so you can use elements from this sub-unit to answer Section C questions about innovation, for example:

1   With reference to an organization of your choice, discuss the impact of **innovation** on operations management **strategy**.   [20]

2   With reference to an organization of your choice, examine the impact of **innovation** on operations management **strategy**.   [20]

3   With reference to an organization of your choice, examine the impact of **innovation** on promotional **strategy**.   [20]

In all these cases, to discuss the concept of innovation, you should refer to materials and ideas from this sub-unit (for example about types of innovation, or advantages and disadvantages of R&D) – this will help you score higher for criterion A, which is described as follows in the IB subject guide:

"This criterion addresses the extent to which the student demonstrates knowledge and understanding of the given concepts and relevant business management content (theories, techniques or tools, depending on the requirements of the question)."

A later section of this book (page 130) develops and illustrates this criterion and the others.

Content link
Link to other sub-units

- Sub-unit 1.3 about organizational objectives covers the strategies of product development and diversification in the Ansoff matrix; these two strategies are linked to the sub-unit, as new products are the result of product innovation.

- Sub-unit 4.5, the P for Product of the marketing mix, about the product life cycle and about extension strategies, is linked to this sub-unit for the same reason, as R&D innovation results in new products.

Content link
Link to your IA

Even if your IA is not about operations management, you could apply the contents of this sub-unit to your chosen organization: where do innovation, research and development take place in your organization? Is there a particular department or group of people responsible for it? Can you give examples of innovations they have implemented over time?

All six concepts are linked to the topic of research and development:

- **Innovation**, because innovation is at the core of R&D (which is why this sub-unit focuses so much on innovation, as innovation and R&D go together).

- **Ethics**, because research is sometimes based on practices that may be regarded as unethical, such as testing of new pharmaceutical drugs and of cosmetics on animals.

- **Strategy**, because R&D can be mentioned in the strategic plan of the organization, especially if it operates in a sector where R&D is particularly important, such as high technology, architecture or fashion; strategically, the entire company could be reliant on its R&D activities.

- **Globalization**, because the largest multinational companies (MNCs) develop new products that are then commercialized on a global scale, from cars to detergents, from clothes to technological devices.

- **Change**, because R&D is an ongoing process of creation, over time, of new products and new systems, ceaselessly changing the portfolio of the goods and services that the organization offers.

- **Culture**, because an organization that wants to define itself as "innovative" will nourish a culture of innovation throughout, in all departments, not solely in the R&D department.

5.7   CRISIS MANAGEMENT AND CONTINGENCY PLANNING (HL ONLY)

This sub-unit focuses on organizations' abilities to deal with severe unpredicted problems.

You should be able to:

✔ distinguish between crisis management and contingency planning

✔ analyse factors that affect effective crisis management

✔ analyse the advantages and disadvantages of contingency planning.

Topic summary

Crisis management is a direct response to a specific, unpredictable event, whereas contingency planning refers to an organization's efforts to minimize the effects of a potential crisis.

The main factors that affect crisis management are:

- Communication from senior managers.

- Transparency: telling stakeholders the truth.

- Speed: in both actions and communication.

- Control of the impacts.

Crisis management needs to be well-communicated, controlled and prompt.

Not every crisis can be anticipated, but contingency planning is about being prepared, in advance, just in case; four factors are important for contingency planning:

- Risks: what risks, to whom, and how likely are they? (This is called "risk assessment" and organizations may prepare a "risk assessment register".)

- Cost: contingency planning may be costly, but less so than dealing with the crisis.

- Time: contingency planning takes time, especially for preparation.

- Safety: contingency planning must put safety first.

>> **Revision tip**

As you revise this sub-unit, you should think of real examples of crises that have recently affected business organizations, either locally, near you, or on a global scale. The different areas of the STEEPLE framework can give you a starting point: it could be a political crisis, an economic crisis, an ecological crisis etc.

Content link
Link to other sub-units

- Sub-unit 2.3 about the key functions of management is linked to this sub-unit, as managers are also responsible for contingency planning and dealing with crises, should they occur.

- Sub-unit 3.9 about budgets is linked to this sub-unit as companies usually set reserve funds aside to deal with any crisis.

- Sub-unit 4.5, the P for Promotion of the marketing mix is linked to this sub-unit, in the way social media can be used to communicate about a product as well as about a crisis.

Content link
Link to your IA

Even if your IA is not about operations management, you could apply the contents of this sub-unit to your chosen organization. Have they been affected by some external or internal crises in the past? Do they have contingency plans? Who is responsible for crisis management and contingency planning?

Concept link

The concepts of **ethics** and **culture** are linked to the topic of crisis management:

- **Ethics**, because stakeholders expect transparency in communication about the crisis (this was an issue in large-scale scandals such as the 2001 Enron accounting fraud and the 2010 BP Deepwater Horizon oil spill).

- **Culture**, because some entrepreneurs may be less interested in contingency planning than in risk-taking, yet good business acumen is about thinking both optimistically and pessimistically about both the best and worst scenarios.

QUESTIONS WORTH 10 MARKS

The task

Besides shorter questions worth 2 marks, 4 marks or 6 marks (the ones that start with command terms such as "define" or "explain"), all your exam papers have *at least* one question worth 10 marks:

- SL paper 1 (Section B, **one** question at the end of question 4, compulsory).

- HL paper 1 (Section B, **one** question at the end of question 4, compulsory).

- SL paper 2 (Section B, at the end of questions 3, 4 and 5; you must answer **two** out of three questions).

- HL paper 2 (Section B, at the end of questions 3, 4 and 5; you must answer **two** out of three questions).

Put another way, you will have to answer **three** questions worth 10 marks – this represents 30 marks in total in your business management exams.

▼ **Table 6.1.1** Examples of questions worth 10 marks

Discuss whether Sam should accept the offer of a takeover.
Discuss two appropriate sources of finance for the renovation of GCK's factories.
Discuss human resources strategies that could reduce the impact on employees of the changes suggested by Mrs K.
Using the Ansoff matrix, evaluate two possible growth strategies for A4A.

These questions have two main features:

1. They always start with command terms such as "discuss", "evaluate" or "examine"; the task is more demanding and your answer will be longer, more structured, more developed.

2. They always refer to some stimulus material and thus to an organization or some of its stakeholders, which is why there are references to "Sam", "GCK", "Mrs K" and "A4A" in the questions shown.

Your answer to such questions is likely to be *at least* one page long, and usually much more in order to achieve a high mark. If your answer is too short, you will not sufficiently develop the different points and arguments.

Because of the breakdown of marks and the time/marks ratio, you should **spend at least 20 minutes** on each of these questions.

Assessment of the questions worth 10 marks: the markbands

The examiners use markbands for these questions, so it is important that you understand the criteria in advance: this way, you know what the examiner expects in your answer.

For these questions, the IB markbands are as follows:

▼ Table 6.1.2 The assessment markbands for questions worth 10 marks

Marks	Level descriptor
0	The work does not reach a standard described by the descriptors below.
1–2	• Little understanding of the demands of the question. • Few business management tools (where applicable), techniques and theory are explained or applied and business management terminology is lacking. • Little reference to the stimulus material.
3–4	• Some understanding of the demands of the question. • Some relevant business management tools (where applicable), techniques and theories are explained or applied, and some appropriate terminology is used. • Some reference to the stimulus material but often not going beyond the name of a person(s) and/or the name of the organization.
5–6	• Understanding of most of the demands of the question. • Relevant business management tools (where applicable), techniques and theories are explained and applied, and appropriate terminology is used most of the time. • Some reference to the stimulus material that goes beyond the name of a person(s) and/or the name of the organization. • Some evidence of a balanced response. • Some judgments are relevant but not substantiated.
7–8	• Good understanding of the demands of the question. • Relevant business management tools (where applicable), techniques and theories are explained and applied well, and appropriate terminology is used. • Good reference to the stimulus material. • Good evidence of a balanced response. • The judgments are relevant but not always well substantiated.
9–10	• Good understanding of the demands of the question, including implications, where relevant. • Relevant business management tools (where applicable), techniques and theories are explained clearly and applied purposefully, and appropriate terminology is used throughout the response. • Effective use of the stimulus material in a way that significantly strengthens the response. • Evidence of balance is consistent throughout the response. • The judgments are relevant and well substantiated.

Source: IB *Business management guide*

QUESTION PRACTICE

Example 1

To highlight the difference between a "good answer" (markband for 7–8 marks) and a "very good answer" (markband for 9–10 marks), we will consider the following question.

The question is about a chain of hotels called *Dales*. In 2010, in order to remain competitive, *Dales* outsourced the cleaning of hotel rooms to a company called *Wire*. Recent customer feedback however has highlighted concerns about room cleanliness at *Dales* hotels – so *Dales* in now considering whether it should stop outsourcing the cleaning service.

Recommend if *Dales* should stop outsourcing the cleaning of hotel rooms.

[10]

>> Assessment tip

To score 9–10 rather than 7–8, you must do the following (as taken from the wording of the 9–10 section of the IB markband):

1 Refer to implications i.e. consequences and impacts. The question here is "Recommend if *Dales* should stop outsourcing the cleaning of hotel rooms"; what would be the implications of stopping the outsourcing and of not stopping the outsourcing? If *Dales* stops outsourcing its cleaners, the costs will rise – very good answers will refer to this!

2 Explain clearly and purposefully the tools, theories and techniques you use in the answer: for example, if you refer to staff turnover rate in your answer, show the examiner why you believe it is a relevant rate to include – because a high turnover rate means high costs for ongoing recruitment and training.

3 Use business terminology all along your response: show the examiner that you can use terms such as "profit", "piece rate system", "recruitment", "competitive environment" and "quality" in your answer.

4 Quote short extracts of the case study to help make a point: here, a very good answer would refer to the fact that "*Dales* is positioned as a high-price and high-quality hotel chain", so guests have very high expectations regarding the cleanliness of the rooms – and insourcing can then help with quality management.

5 Ensure your entire answer is balanced: balanced not only regarding the arguments for and against stopping outsourcing, but also balancing quantitative and qualitative elements, and in this case finance versus human resources.

6 Justify all your judgments: provide evidence and justification for all the points that you make, using both elements from the case study (quoting them) as well as your knowledge of business management – in this case: the advantages and disadvantages of outsourcing.

SAMPLE STUDENT ANSWER

The following answer is therefore a **very good answer**, achieving a mark in the markband for 9–10 marks.

Note: in the commentary provided here, the numbers 1 to 6 refer to the numbers given in the accompanying assessment tip.

Dales hotels have several problems of brand image and reputation: customers are not happy with customer service, food quality and room cleanliness – and all this explains why room booking and profit have decreased so much. To address the issue of room cleanliness, *Dales* could decide to stop subcontracting to Wire – and to "insource" this service again.

Option 1: *Dales* stops outsourcing

On the one hand, if Dales stops outsourcing its cleaners, costs will rise, as outsourcing did cut costs (from 5% of room revenues to 2%) – so insourcing would be more expensive, both for the variable costs (per room) and fixed costs too (the costs of recruiting and training cleaners). These costs may be even higher, as the high staff turnover rate amongst cleaners means that recruitment and training would be ongoing. In the short term, this means that Dales' overall profit (which is already low) would be hit (and may even turn into loss). On the other hand, the quality of room cleanliness may improve, and Dales would be able to control this, training its own cleaners to the right standards, without relying on Wire's own systems and practices, which are below Dales' benchmarks. This is a problem as Dales is "positioned as a high-price and high-quality chain" so in the luxury market where guests are very demanding.

▲ This is a reference to implications (1).

▲ The tools used are explained (2).

▲ Use of subject terminology all along (3).

▲ Short extracts of the case study are quoted to help make a point (4).

Option 2: *Dales* continues outsourcing

Financially, outsourcing has enabled Dales to save some money, which is very important at this moment in time, when bookings are going down. If finance is the priority, outsourcing is the best strategy, but Dales' managers should speak to Wire about the declining quality and guests' complaints. The cleaners employed by Wire must work to satisfy Dales' hotel guests, as Dales is their customer – or Dales could contact other cleaning companies and see how much it would cost, and whether they would provide better service. There may be other local companies offering the same services as Wire.

▲ Balanced arguments all along (5).

In conclusion, we can see that both options have advantages and disadvantages. Insourcing may seem a good idea, but it will only solve one of Dales' problems; there are other factors that contribute to the falling room occupancy rate: the quality of food and the quality of customer service. Dales should adopt a total quality management approach in order to make improvements in all areas, and not just consider the cleanliness as an isolated factor.

▲ The judgments are substantiated, using both data from the case study and knowledge from the business syllabus (6).

This response could have achieved 9/10 marks.

Example 2

To apply the generic markband to a specific question, we will consider the following question.

The case study here is about Sam's small business that successfully sells fair trade products in some stores and via e-commerce. The extra material, at the start of Section B, refers to the fact that Sam has been offered a takeover by a very large international retailer.

Discuss whether Sam should accept the offer of a takeover. [10]

▶▶ Assessment tip

In order to score 9 or 10 marks, you need to do the following:

IB criteria from the 9–10 markband	What this means for this question:
	"Discuss whether Sam should accept the offer of a takeover."
Good understanding of the demands of the question, including implications, where relevant.	You must show that you understand the task well… and that you do what the question is requiring you to do.
	The command term "discuss" means "offer a considered and balanced review that includes a range of arguments, factors or hypotheses. Opinions or conclusions should be presented clearly and supported by appropriate evidence".
	Here you are asked to weigh up the reasons why Sam should accept the takeover versus the reasons why he should not accept it.
Relevant business management tools (where applicable), techniques and theories are explained clearly and applied purposefully, and appropriate terminology is used throughout the response.	You must show that you know the meaning of "takeover" (a form of acquisition) as well as the advantages and disadvantages of a takeover as a method of external growth, and the associated risks. In your answer, you are likely to use relevant terms from other parts of the syllabus, especially from "1.6 Growth and evolution" about takeover – for example you could write about organizational structure, workers' motivation and stakeholder conflict (as a takeover may lead to some issues regarding human resources management). When you plan your answer and write draft notes, consider the *entire* course, not just the topic of the question (here: takeover).
Effective use of the stimulus material in a way that significantly strengthens the response.	In the case of paper 1, this means that you must use both the pre-release case study and the unseen extra material at the start of question 4. The word "effective" means that you must not just copy passages from it in your answer, but you must select relevant ideas and integrate them in your answer. This is *not* an exercise of reading comprehension: the examiner is not going to assess if you can spot, in the text, the passages where relevant arguments are made. You may, of course, quote the stimulus, but this alone is not enough: remember, the examiner has the same text, and they will not give you extra marks just because you can quote it.

Evidence of balance is consistent throughout the response.	Write a *balanced* answer: for all these "discuss" questions, there are always arguments for and against (here: reasons for the takeover, reasons against the takeover). For high marks, the examiner expects you to consider both sides. This does not mean that you will have the exact same number of arguments – for example, you could conclude that there are more arguments *against* the takeover than arguments *for* the takeover, and thus that Sam should *not* accept the takeover…or the other way around!
	Such "discuss" questions usually do not have a right or wrong answer; what the examiner will reward is your ability to consider different perspectives, evaluate arguments and come up with a clear, specific, explicit conclusion.
The judgments are relevant and well substantiated.	All the points you make in your answer should be **directly linked** to the question (here: the takeover) and **justified** (i.e. providing reasons, not just statements).
	As part of your exam preparation, you may have prepared mock answers about leadership styles and you want to show the examiner that you know about them…but should you write about this? Yes, if you can link it to the topic of takeover (for example about the fact that the takeover would end the conflict between Sam's and Finn's leadership styles, as Sam would then be selling the business and leaving *AFA*). If, however, you cannot make a link, it is better not to write about it.
	Your judgments must be relevant – and also substantiated: this means that they must be justified, validated, corroborated, with reference to the case study and to your knowledge of business management, in an objective way.

SAMPLE STUDENT ANSWER

The following very good answer achieved full marks:

From the *AFA's* perspective, selling *AFA* to a very large international retailer with a strong online presence is able to increase *AFA's* brand image and become more popular than before. A larger international retailer means that they have a better source of finance so that it can help *AFA* bigger in the market. It also means that the retailer has a better managing system to help *AFA* to deal with the managerial problems. In addition, it might be able to help *AFA* to deal with the problem of decreasing gross profit margin. Also, the diseconomies of scale may be able to sort out by the large international retailer as they have a wider way to reach suppliers and they have a better ability to do bulk buying. As a whole, it will help *AFA* to grow and expand to a better stage and increase the brand reputation.

▲ The candidate does not simply repeat what is in the stimulus material (for example about the strong online presence of the international retailer) but also makes deductions about what it means (for example in terms of source of finance and management systems).

▲ The candidate uses relevant subject terminology throughout, for example about "decreasing gross profit margin" and "diseconomies of scale".

However, all the advantages above are just an assumption. There is not so much information about the international retailer except a strong online presence. Is it selling for trade products? Does the managing system actually fit AFA's situation? Is the brand image of AFA able to remain by the new retailer? These are problems that Sam needs to think about carefully.

▲ The candidate considers the issue from different perspectives, as different stakeholders may have different views. This approach often works very well.

From Sam's perspective, right now there are huge disagreements between Sam and Finn which is not good to the AFA operation. Sam's leadership style is totally different from Finn's and from the case study, it seems that Sam is not able to work well with Finn. This will also demotivate other employees are well. Therefore takeover can be one of the strategies to sort out the communication problems as Sam is no longer the leader of AFA. On the other hand, takeover can provide Sam a great deal of finance so that he can invest in other areas that he is interested in. Before there was a financial problem when Sam first started up his business, but now it won't be.

▲ The candidate provides a balanced view, for example about both the disadvantages and the advantages for Sam.

In this case, Sam is able to have enough fresh capital to start new innovative businesses, as well as put the Daniel Pink theory into the new business as this theory almost failed in AFA. Other than this, the business growth was outstripping Sam and Finn's ability to manage which means Sam not actually fully capable of managing AFA. Taking over AFA by others can help Sam out.

▲ The candidate analyses the consequences of the different courses of action: writing "which means" is a good device to make links between ideas and to show the examiner that the candidate understands the different implications of business decisions.

However, this is the first business for Sam and he has put a lot of efforts for AFA's growth. Right now even the gross profit margin is declining but it is still acceptable. On the other hand, even though Sam sometimes has disagreements with Finn, the business still runs pretty well, at least it is growing. The future of AFA is unknown and if it is not good, it will be bad news for Sam if he accepts the offer of takeover.

▲ The candidate uses suitable terms such as "however" and "on the other hand" which enable them to contrast ideas, to fully discuss them, as opposed to writing a one-sided answer.

From the employees' perspective, taking over is not good now for them as they might be fired, especially for Finn and Kim who also put a lot of efforts in AFA.

▲ The candidate pursues the logic of the structure they decided to give in the answer, i.e. considering different perspectives one after the other (from the manager's perspective, from the employees' perspective, from the customers' perspective…) This is also fully in line with the IB learner profile.

However from the customer's perspective, this may be beneficial as the price of the fair trade products might be likely to decrease as AFA will be able to reach economies of scale and hence reduce the price.

Overall, Sam should accept the offer as the advantages outweigh the disadvantages. Right now AFA is facing many problems, financial, managerial as well as the serving quality of the retail shops. The leaders of AFA seem not able to deal with all the problems and it should be better for AFA to pass on to the large international retailer for a better future and market share.

▲ The conclusion is clear and explicit: more advantages than disadvantages, so Sam should accept the offer (the opposite conclusion, not accepting the offer, would have been acceptable too, depending on the factors and elements emphasized by the candidate).

This response could have achieved 10/10 marks.

Note: The answer fulfils all the criteria for a maximum mark of 10/10. This does not mean that the answer is perfect – for example the candidate could have written more about the conflict between Sam and Finn – however the examiner is not waiting for the perfect, ultimate, fully comprehensive answer in order to award 10/10, especially given the time constraints of the exam conditions.

EXTENDED RESPONSES (SECTION C)

The task

"Extended responses" are worth **20 marks** each, and so contribute greatly to the final mark. They are not about a specific point in the syllabus (such as the definition of a business term or the calculation of a financial ratio) but they are **holistic**: this means that your answer must combine different parts of the course so you can show your knowledge and understanding of business management at a more general level. This is in line with the first aim of the IB business management course, as written in the guide: "to encourage a holistic view of the world of business".

Another key difference with shorter responses (i.e. answers to questions using command terms such as "describe" or "explain") is the fact that your answer will be much longer and clearly structured as an **essay**, with an introduction, a main body composed of several paragraphs and a conclusion.

- **SL students** answer one extended response, in Section C of paper 2, focusing on **two** of the six concepts (culture, change, ethics, globalization, innovation, strategy) integrating relevant content of the syllabus. You must answer this question with reference to a real-world organization of your choice.

- **HL students** answer two extended responses: Section C of paper 1 and Section C of paper 2. There are two differences between them:

  ○ Your answer to paper 1 Section C is about the fictional, pre-released paper 1 case study, whereas your answer to paper 2 Section C is about a real-world organization of your choice.

  ○ Your answer to paper 2 Section C is focused on two of the six concepts (culture, change, ethics, globalization, innovation, strategy) integrating relevant content of the syllabus, whereas your answer to paper 1 Section C is *only* about the content of the syllabus (so not about the concepts).

Section C of paper 2 (both SL and HL)

Examples of questions

Section C (HL)

Answer **one** question from this section. The organizations featured in Sections A and B in the paper 1 case study may not be used as a basis to your answer.

6. With reference to an organization of your choice, examine the impact of **innovation** on promotional **strategy**. [20]

7. With reference to an organization of your choice, examine the impact of **globalization** on **change** in operations management. [20]

8. With reference to an organization of your choice, examine the impact of **ethics** and **culture** on human resource management. [20]

Section C (SL)

Answer **one** question from this section. The organizations featured in Sections A and B and in the paper 1 case study may not be used as a basis to your answer.

6. With reference to an organization of your choice, examine the impact of **globalization** on **innovation**. [20]

7. With reference to an organization of your choice, examine the impact of **ethics** on organizational **strategy**. [20]

8. With reference to an organization of your choice, discuss the ways in which **culture** can promote or inhibit **change**. [20]

▼ **Table 7.1.1** Four characteristics the questions always have

They always ask you to write about **one organization of your choice.**	It is essential that you prepare *at least* one case study in depth, so that you know in advance, before the exam, about which organization you will write in your extended response. Choosing a suitable organization, researching it in depth, and memorizing what you have studied about it, before the exam, is part of your exam preparation.
They always start with an **evaluative command term** such as "discuss" or "examine".	Although there is a slight difference between these command terms, the expectation is similar. You must synthetize and evaluate, i.e. bring together different elements and arguments in order to reach a conclusion at the end of your essay. Depending on the command term and the question, you could be asked to write about contrasting aspects (such as advantages and disadvantages) or to explore an issue in depth (for example considering causes and consequences, or short-term impacts and long-term impacts).
They always focus on **two** of the six **concepts**.	You are given a choice of three questions, so you do not need to be equally strong on all six concepts. If, for example, ethics is a topic that you find difficult, you can still do very well for the exam – by avoiding the question about ethics.
They always include **course contents.**	In your answer, you need to show your knowledge of the different units of the course. Depending on the topic, you could write about elements of the marketing mix, or about factors that influence oragnizational growth, or about human resources and operations. The questions are not just about the concepts: they also assess your knowledge and understanding of business management, like the rest of the exam and your IA.

The assessment criteria

The criteria are always the same, so you know in advance how you will be assessed, that is, what the examiner will want to see in your answer and how they will mark it. The approach is similar to IAs, with criteria and "markbands".

The examiner will mark your extended response using five criteria, A to E:

- **Criterion A** assesses your knowledge and understanding of the course contents and of the concepts.
- **Criterion B** assesses your ability to apply the course contents and concepts to your chosen organization.
- **Criterion C** assesses your ability to make reasoned arguments, responding to the evaluative command term.
- **Criterion D** assesses your ability to structure your answer and organize your ideas.
- **Criterion E** assesses your ability to refer to a range of stakeholders (both individuals and groups).

Criterion A (up to 4 marks)

To achieve a high mark for Criterion A, you need to show your knowledge and understanding of the two **concepts** in the question (for example "ethics" and "strategy") **and** of the course **content** you will refer to in your answer (for example about corporate social responsibility, organizational objectives and triple bottom line). You should also use business terminology throughout your answer: you want to show the examiner that you have studied IB business management and that in your response, you are able to incorporate subject-specific terms such as "mission statement" and "stakeholders".

Criterion B (up to 4 marks)

To achieve a high mark for Criterion B, you must **apply** your theoretical knowledge (assessed through Criterion A) to an organization of your choice. Your application must be **precise,** with specific data and facts, possibly even names, dates, numbers, quotes, so not just generic and vague examples. It is therefore essential that you memorize facts, data and details about your chosen organization. As part of your preparation, you should apply all models from the course (from SWOT analysis to the Ansoff matrix) to your chosen organization, and learn about all aspects, from human resources to operations, from marketing to finance. If your knowledge of your organization is too superficial, you will not be able to achieve top marks for Criterion B.

Criterion C (up to 4 marks)

To achieve a high mark for Criterion C, you need to respond to the **evaluative** command term ("examine" or "discuss") and to make reasoned arguments. Depending on the focus of question, this could mean: exploring and contrasting different practices or perspectives, weighing up strengths and weaknesses, or advantages and disadvantages, or short-term impacts versus long-term impacts and implications. It is important that you justify your judgments, providing evidence; knowing facts, data and details about number of employees, size, turnover, strategic direction, structure, internal strengths and weaknesses, external opportunities and threats will help you make reasoned judgments.

Criterion D (up to 4 marks)

To achieve a high mark for Criterion D, you need to:

- **Organize your ideas** clearly (for example one section about advantages, then one section about disadvantages).

- **Structure your answer** with an introduction, a main body (composed of coherent and logical paragraphs) and a conclusion.

Many students fail to score the full 4 marks for Criterion D simply because they do not follow a clear structure. For example, they write big blocks of text without any paragraphs and don't show much effort in terms of layout and presentation. You should leave blank lines between your paragraphs to help the examiner see the structure of your answer, and you should signpost your conclusion with an expression such as "in conclusion..." or "to conclude..." – this way, the examiner will readily give you 4 marks for Criterion D.

Criterion E (up to 4 marks)

To achieve a high mark for Criterion E, you must refer to a range of **stakeholders** in your answer, both individuals (such as the founder, a manager or a specific employee) and groups (such as the workers, the customers or the suppliers). There is no expectation regarding the number of stakeholders – but you should include both **internal** ones and **external** ones (this is also a good way to show that you know the difference between them). As so many people may be considered as stakeholders (including the local community and the government), it should not be difficult to think of stakeholders that may be affected by the activities and decisions of an organization. You could decide to refer to stakeholders throughout your answer, or you may prefer to keep this for a specific section in your essay, for example towards the end. This is up to you; what matters is that you give balanced consideration to a range of relevant stakeholders.

▼ **Table 7.1.2** Five tips for your extended response

1	How long should you spend on your extended response questions? Paper 2 at standard level lasts 105 minutes for 50 marks, which comes down to 2 minutes per mark; on this basis, you should spend *at least* 40 minutes on Section C. In practice, you are likely to spend even more, as for example a "define" question worth 2 marks never takes 4 minutes to answer. You should spend at least 45 minutes on your extended response.
2	Do not start writing straightaway: plan your answer, both in terms of structure and contents. In your rough notes, you could write down some notes and key words such as "E: stakeholders" so you do not forget to write about stakeholders (Criterion E) – or "paragraphs" so you do not neglect the visual appearance and layout of your answer (Criterion D). It is easy to achieve high marks for Criteria D and E, but it is also easy to forget them.
3	How many words should you write, how long should your answer be? What matters is not the *quantity but the quality* of your answer. This said, if your answer is too short, just one page long, it probably will not address all five Criteria A to E. Good answers are usually at least three pages long, although this may depend on the size of your handwriting.

| 4 | The choice of your organization is essential. You may have discussed with your teacher which organization you will choose. Remember that you know so many examples and case studies:
- The ones you have studied in class.
- Your IA topic (and maybe the IA topics of your friends).
- Organizations you may refer to in your extended essay (if you wrote it in business management).
- Local businesses, maybe your family business.
There are many other possible organizations, such as non-profit making organizations that your CAS project may be linked to, your school (and school-based ventures or social enterprise clubs), as well as a church or sports clubs you may belong to.
Consider charities, NGOs, political parties: they too are organizations in their own right, they deal with issues of change, strategy, culture, ethics, innovation and globalization.
In business management classes, we often tend to refer to "business organizations" strictly speaking (e.g. McDonald's, Starbucks, Apple…), but the focus is not just on businesses: all types of businesses are valid, all types of organizations are valid. Without realizing it, you know a lot of examples. |
|---|---|
| 5 | Remember that your answer is a vehicle of **communication**. The pages will be scanned and read on screen by an examiner who will have to scroll up and down. An answer which is not easy to read, because of poor handwriting, is unlikely to make a good impression; the examiner will not spend time trying to decipher what you have written. If you think that your handwriting is sometimes illegible, make sure that, during the exam, you write slowly and clearly. |

QUESTION PRACTICE

With reference to an organization of your choice, examine the impact of **ethics** on organizational **strategy**. [20]

▲ Although it is not required to define the two concepts in the introduction, it is good practice as it can help the candidate stay focused – and show the examiner that they know what these two concepts mean, even in generic terms (Criterion A).

▲ In the introduction, it is important to present the company, even if it is a well-known MNC such as Tesla here (or Starbucks or McDonald's). A couple of sentences are enough.

▲ In the introduction the candidate shows their knowledge of business management, about a "mission statement", and of their chosen company, Tesla, as they quote their mission statement (Criteria A and B).

▲ The extended response is not just about concepts; the candidate shows here that they know the course contents too – in this case: the marketing mix, starting with a reference to the P of Place (Criterion A).

Ethics is a set of morals that an organization follows. Although ethics is subjective, most people have a similar sense of what is ethically correct and what is ethically incorrect. Strategies are plans and goals a business has to achieve their long-term aims. Ethics plays a hug role on organizational strategy. Tesla Motors Inc. is a public limited company headquartered in California, United States. They operate mainly in the automotive sector. Tesla is known worldwide for its electric powered cars. Their mission statement is to accelerate the world's transition to clean energy, and they are doing so by producing environmentally safe cars. Ethics plays a huge role in Tesla's strategy.

Ethics can be seen in strategies such as Tesla's marketing mix. For place, they don't use dealerships. This is because they want better service for their consumers. They know consumers get frustrated with salespeople not giving them the right price on a car, so they have decided not to use dealerships, but instead use

B2C e-commerce, and have showrooms so consumers can see the car before purchasing. This promotes the social aspect of the triple bottom line because Tesla wants consumers to feel better about the car they're buying. Then there's product. This is important because Tesla's product the Model S is an environmentally friendly electric car. This is an innovative car, that has all the luxury features of a car, such as a Mercedes-Benz, but also has the feature of being environmentally friendly. Tesla's strategy of choosing this specific car is ethical in two ways. One, it helps to save the environment, and provides consumers with the choice of saving the environment. Second, this correlates directly with their missions of transitioning the world to sustainable energy.

On the other hand, elements such as price might not seem to go with their ethical viewpoint. The price on their Model S ranges from $60 000 USD to around $120 000 USD. This seems to go against Tesla's goal of bringing the whole world to use sustainable energy, as most of the world can't afford the car. It seems very unethical that Tesla would make such a high-end car that nobody can afford, when they could've made a lower-end car so more people can afford it. However, this strategy is indeed ethical, even though it might not seem like it. Tesla's master plan has been on their website for a few years, before they started working on production of the Model S. In it the CEO, Elon Musk, stated that he would sell a mid-range car for a lower price than the Tesla Roadster they were selling at the time, which turned out to be the Model S. He also stated he would build a mid-range car at a lower price, which is the Model 3 that Tesla is focused on making. This will cost around $35 000, which many more people can afford. So in the end, Tesla and Musk are staying true to their mission even though it might not seem like it. This strategy, of starting with higher-end rather than mass market cars was necessary for Tesla's survival. The automotive industry is hard to start-up in, and a mass market car wouldn't give Tesla the profit margins needed to survive. So by building an environmentally friendly innovative car, Tesla ensured they could start-up in the industry. Therefore, Tesla's long-term strategy is ethical, and it is because of Musk's personal ethics that the strategy is like that.

▲ The candidate shows that they know about Tesla's practice – in this case: their use of showrooms (Criterion B).

▲ The candidate integrates another element from the course in their answer: the triple bottom line (Criterion A).

▲ The candidate makes reasoned judgments (Criterion C).

▲ The structure of the answer is clear, with a counter-argument presented here, with "on the other hand" (Criterion D).

▲ The candidate uses precise information to answer the question, here about the prices of the Model S Tesla car (Criterion B).

▲ The evaluation is precise and justified: "seems very unethical" (Criterion C).

▲ Elon Musk, as CEO, is a key individual stakeholder (Criterion E).

▲ The analysis is well thought out (Criterion C).

▲ Another specific reference to one of the organization's strategies (Criterion B).

Another strategy Tesla has is they put all excess cash flow back into the business for R&D. This shows Elon Musk's ethics and morals and how they shape Tesla's strategy. Since Musk wants Tesla to become more innovative, he ploughs all cash flow back into the business, and doesn't take any for himself. This shows how much Musk cares for the triple bottom line, as he doesn't take cash flow for himself.

▲ The candidate links "theory" and "practice" very well in their evaluation (Criteria A, B, C).

▲ Another specific reference to one of the organization's strategies (Criterion B).

Another strategy Tesla is working on, is the production of its Gigafactory. The strategic building of this facility will allow Tesla to use economies of scale to their benefit, and will allow them to produce the Model 3 quicker, and more ethically. Ethics shaped the reasoning behind this strategy. As Tesla is an ethical company, they want to make sure everything is produced ethically. So the Gigafactory will run on solar panels and sustainable energy so Tesla can provide the world access to sustainable cars, but also be ethical in the way they produce them. Most of the car will be built in the factory to ensure that Tesla stays true to its ethics. Although one can argue that this is just for marketing purposes and Tesla isn't as ethical as it seems, Tesla has had a huge history of being ethical, with the CEO being very adamant on changing how we use energy, so there are minimal signs of greenwashing.

▲ The candidate integrates the vocabulary of business management very well throughout their answer, here about "economies of scale" (Criterion A).

▲ The candidate duly focuses on the two concepts of ethics and strategy throughout their answer (Criterion A).

▲ The candidate uses their knowledge of the company (here their use of solar panels) to substantiate their judgment about how Tesla's strategic decisions are underpinned by ethics (Criteria A, B, C).

▲ The candidate uses subject terminology throughout, here about marketing and "greenwashing" (Criterion A).

Many stakeholders are affected by Tesla's ethics and ethical strategy. One, there are the consumers, which are happy with the products they receive and are very happy to be part of making the world more green. Although some potential consumers called "motorheads" won't buy the car because it's not gas powered, this is a very small minority. Another stakeholder is CEO Elon Musk. Musk has a very strong opinion on sustainable energy and this is shown through his company. He is interested in not only the wellbeing of his company, but also that of the world. This is what makes him different from other CEOs and what makes Tesla such an ethical company.

▲ Although they already referred to some of the stakeholders (especially the CEO), the candidate decided to add one section specifically about other stakeholders (Criterion E).

▲ The conclusion is well signposted, and all the other paragraphs (including the introduction) were clearly identifiable (Criterion D). It also recaps the main arguments made, showing how well the candidate focused on the demands of the question (Criterion C).

In conclusion, as shown through examples of Tesla, ethics has a very important role in strategy. It plays a role on the marketing mix of a company, how they carry on with day to day operations, how they plan new infrastructure, and even the mission statement of the business. The ethics of the CEO and consumers thus have a huge impact on strategy, and directly impact how a business is run.

Criterion A	4/4	The candidate understands both concepts very well (ethics and strategy) and they also show an excellent command of business management (for example through references to the marketing mix, economies of scale and the triple bottom line).
Criterion B	4/4	All the theoretical points are duly applied to the chosen organization (Tesla) which the candidate clearly knows very well.
Criterion C	4/4	The argument is very clear, though maybe too one-sided; the candidate could have been more critical about Tesla and its ethical statements – the examiner hesitated in choosing between 3 and 4 marks.
Criterion D	4/4	The answer is well presented, from introduction to conclusion, with clear paragraphs and a logical flow and structure.
Criterion E	4/4	The candidate refers to several stakeholders – both internal and external, and both individual(s) and group(s).
Total	**20/20**	This is an excellent answer in all respects.

This response could have achieved 20/20 marks.

Section C of paper 1 (HL only)

There are very few differences between Section C of paper 1 and Section C of paper 2:

- The concepts are not assessed in paper 1, so Criterion A is slightly different: it does not assess *both* conceptual understanding and knowledge of the course contents, but *only* knowledge of the course contents.

- The organization is the fictional case study, like the rest of paper 1. The organization used as a case study for all of the questions in paper 1, is fictional.

All other aspects are the same: Criteria B, C, D, E; recommended time at least 40 minutes.

INTERNAL ASSESSMENT

Internal assessment at standard level

Your task

Your IA task at standard level (referred to as the IA task at SL) is a written commentary: you have to write a commentary (in 1500 words maximum) applying tools, theories, techniques and terminology from the course in order to answer a research question about a contemporary issue faced by a business organization. Your IA must be based on three to five supporting documents that you use, analyse, combine and synthesize, in order to reach your conclusions, hence the name commentary. Supporting documents are typically articles from business news, extracts of a company's official documents, such as their annual report, or publications by organizations such as governments or NGOs. The format of the IA task at SL is close to the "essay" format of writing that you are familiar with, as opposed to the "report" format of the IA task at HL. The aim of the task is that you engage with a contemporary business issue, and with recent authentic business documents.

Examples of recent titles

Should Tesla build its Gigafactory 3 in China to improve profitability?	This is a **good** research question because it may be possible to answer the question precisely ("yes" or "no"), after considering different stakeholders' perspectives presented in three to five documents. The research question suggests that the following business tools, theories and techniques may be used: financial analysis (especially profitability ratios) and PEST analysis of China (as a suitable location, or not, for the project).
Could the introduction of tea-based drinks by Starbucks benefit its growth in China?	This is a **good** research question because it may be possible to answer the question precisely ("yes" or "no"), after considering different stakeholders' perspectives presented in three to five documents. The research question suggests that the following business tools, theories and techniques may be used: perception map of Starbucks in India, SWOT analysis, Ansoff matrix.
Investigation of whether Netflix will remain profitable with their current business model in Europe in the long run.	This is **not** a good research question for two reasons. Firstly, it is not worded as a question. The topic is interesting and has potential, but it should be worded in such a way that an answer could be reached at the end, for example "Could Netflix remain profitable in Europe in the long run with their current business model?" Secondly, the choice of Europe implies that the candidate considers Europe as an entity, yet the success of Netflix is likely to vary across Europe, in different European countries.
Can Starbucks still survive in the future?	This is **not** a good research question because it is too broad. Is the candidate referring to their own country? Or to the USA where Starbucks started and has its highest number of coffee shops? Or to the entire world? Starbucks operates in more than 70 countries, with very different market conditions, so the research question should be more focused.

The assessment criteria

Your teacher will mark your IA using seven criteria, A to G:

- Criterion A assesses your choice of supporting documents.
- Criterion B assesses your choice and application of business tools, techniques and theories.
- Criterion C assesses your choice and analysis of data (from your supporting documents) and the way you integrate your ideas.
- Criterion D assesses the conclusions you reach at the end of your IA.
- Criterion E assesses your ability to evaluate the arguments and ideas in your IA.
- Criterion F assesses the structure of your IA.
- Criterion G assesses the presentation of your work.

Criterion A: Supporting documents (up to 4 marks)

To achieve a high mark for A, your supporting documents must be relevant, sufficiently in-depth and provide a range of ideas and views that will help you answer your research question. Make sure you spend time choosing them: your first choice might not be the best one! You do not need to carry out primary research for your written commentary, unlike HL students for their internal assessment task; it is often better just to use secondary data. If your documents are in a different language, you must translate the passages that you are using and quoting. You must also ensure that these documents have been recently published, less than three years before the date of submission of your IA to the IB (for example, if your IA is submitted in March 2020, the documents must be published between March 2017 and March 2020).

Criterion B: Choice and application of business tools, techniques and theories (up to 5 marks)

To achieve a high mark for B, you must choose appropriate tools, techniques and theories from the course, and you must apply them skilfully to your chosen organization. The words "tools, techniques and theories" refer to the contents of the curriculum, for example SWOT analysis, Ansoff matrix or the marketing mix, as well as subject terminology, i.e. the correct use of terms such as "stakeholders", "franchising", "mergers and acquisitions", "sources of finance" etc. As an SL candidate, you are allowed to use contents from the HL extension of the course, for example the extended marketing (people, process and physical evidence), if appropriate. Make sure that your models are relevant and suitable: many candidates do a SWOT analysis; this is fine in some cases, but not always! A SWOT analysis could help you better understand your chosen organization, but it may not help you answer your research question. You could include it in appendix, and in the main body, you could quote relevant extracts from it. Tools solely used in the appendix cannot be rewarded though: only the analysis and application of ideas in the main body can be rewarded, so think carefully about the most appropriate tools for your research question.

Criterion C: Choice and analysis of data and integration of ideas (up to 5 marks)

To achieve a high mark for C, you must select relevant data from your supporting documents (for example facts, figures, quotes), analyse them (using your chosen tools, see Criterion B above) and integrate your findings coherently. This last point, integration, means that you must not successively write about supporting document 1, then supporting document 2, then supporting document 3, but you must synthesize and combine them.

Criterion D: Conclusions (up to 3 marks)

To achieve a high mark for D, your conclusion must explicitly answer your research question. It must be consistent with the evidence that you have presented, with your analysis and with your findings. If you have contrasting arguments, this is where you can weigh them up, for example advantages versus disadvantages, in order to reach a precise answer. This is why closed questions ("should company x do y?") are often better for an IA, because the answer will be clear: "Yes…" or "No…."; open questions (such as "to what extent…") are harder to answer in 1500 words; they are better for an extended essay. Your conclusion must also summarize your findings but not add new ideas or new arguments. It should not be too short and too superficial; its length should be a good paragraph or two, up to half a page.

Criterion E: Evaluation (up to 4 marks)

To achieve a high mark for E, you must evaluate the arguments that you present in your commentary, and you must provide evidence to justify your judgments. This will come from your critical thinking skills and from your objective assessment of the supporting documents (for example you could comment on the fact that some documents are biased, or that they represent only some stakeholders' views). If your conclusion is based on a small number of sources, you could show your awareness of the limitation of your work.

Criterion F: Structure (up to 2 marks)

To achieve a high mark for F, the structure of your IA should be appropriate and easy to follow, for example "Part 1: reasons in favour of the merger of companies A and B", followed by "Part 2: reasons against the merger of the two companies". There is no prescribed structure for the IA at standard level, unlike the IA at higher level. The structure of your commentary will depend on the research question, but it must be coherent, logical and easy to follow.

Criterion G: Presentation (up to 2 marks)

To achieve a high mark for G, your work should be well presented. Several formal and structural elements must be present: a title page, an accurate table of contents, appropriate headings and sub-headings, consistent referencing (on the pages themselves, which could be with footnotes or in-text citation), a complete bibliography (which shows the sources of your supporting documents, and indicates other sources that you may have used) and numbered pages. It is important that you make the layout look professional and "business-like": ensure that you submit a document to the IB which has a high standard of presentation and reflects well on you, as a student of business management.

Grade boundaries

The grade boundaries for the IA task at SL are as follows:

Grade	1	2	3	4	5	6	7
Mark range	0–3	4–6	7–9	10–12	13–16	17–19	20–25

This shows you that to score a 7 you do not need to achieve top marks for all the criteria!

Five tips for your IA

1. Make sure that you have three, four or five supporting documents: not less, not more. Every year, some candidates lose marks because they do not have the right number of supporting documents. If you have only one or two, or more than five, you will score only 1 mark for Criterion A, no matter how useful and relevant they are.

2. Label your supporting documents clearly, indicate their sources, and highlight the passages that you are using directly in your commentary. Make sure that you prepare a separate file with these supporting documents. For your IA, you must submit two files to your school: one with your commentary itself (from the cover page and table of contents, to the bibliography and appendices, if you have appendices) and one with the supporting documents.

3. Read the instructions in the IB *Business management guide*, for example about word count: the table of contents and the bibliography do not count, and neither do in-text citations and footnotes, so you may be able to write more than you think. Do not try to go around the word length by creating tables (for example around a SWOT analysis) claiming that the words inside the table do not count because there is a frame around them. Teachers and IB moderators are instructed to stop reading after 1500 words, so you could end up with zero marks for your conclusion (Criterion D) if your conclusion falls beyond the 1500 words limit, as it simply would not be read and marked.

4. Start your conclusion by copying the research question: this will help you ensure that you answer it precisely! Every year, many candidates achieve 2 marks rather than 3 marks for Criterion D because their conclusion does not precisely answer the question they have formulated. Their conclusion is on the same topic, but they have deviated from their original question and did not correct this.

5. Large companies (about which there are articles in the media, such as McDonald's, Starbucks or Uber) are most suitable for the IA task at standard level, unlike the IA task at higher level, where small local ones are often better. When you chose your company, ask yourself whether you will be able to access external documents about it, for example business news. You may then realize that your initial choice, however interesting, for example your parents' business, is not suitable for your written commentary.

Business management standard level

▲ On the cover page, you should mention your research question – as well as basic information such as your course and session, but not your name or school name.

● To what extent will Brexit affect Burberry's penetration of the Chinese market?

▲ 1500 words is the word limit; you may be penalized if you exceed the word limit: teachers and moderators are instructed to stop reading once the word limit is reached, which means that your conclusion may not be read and marked, thus achieving a lower mark for Criterion D.

Session: May 2018

● Word count: 1498

▲ The table of contents is well presented (Criterion G).

The candidate indicates here which tools they are going to use (SWOT, PEST, Ansoff); this relates to Criterion B.

●**Table of contents**

<u>To what extent will Brexit affect Burberry's penetration of the Chinese market?</u>

Introduction

A distinct check pattern; brown, black, white, red and a charging equestrian knight. These are instantaneously recognizable symbols of Burberry. Founded in 1856, it is an iconic British luxury fashion brand. Burberry appeals to customers through its methodology, combining its roots with innovation, leading it to be ranked the 83rd brand worldwide.[1] They operate based on three key values, "Protect, Explore, Inspire", and continue to uphold the brand name.[2] While Burberry's revenue growth was –2%, they boasted a revenue of £2,766 million, much from the Asia-Pacific Region led by the emerging Chinese market (Supporting Document 2). This market is relatively untapped compared to its potential, with a population of 1.3 billion people and high GDP growth rate.

Meanwhile, in Britain, a large political/economic move has taken place, namely, Britain's exit (Brexit) from the European Union (EU). Brexit will happen in March 2019 and will consist of political/economic freedom from the EU; i.e., Britain will become an independent economy. This is because the EU operates under a single market, merging the economies of member countries for easy trading. With the announcement of Britain's departure, the value of the pound fell, remaining around 10% lower against the US dollar. However, the weak pound, with several other factors caused by Brexit, can be an opportunity for businesses, especially in the luxury industry, like Burberry. Therefore, I decided to investigate:

To what extent will Brexit affect Burberry's penetration of the Chinese market?

This commentary will discuss to what extent Brexit will affect Burberry's penetration of the Chinese market. Burberry's Annual Report for 2016/17, a luxury industry overview by Deloitte, a report from the BBC detailing Brexit, an article on China's middle class by McKinsey & Company, and an article from Digiday detailing Burberry's digital innovation will be used as a basis. A SWOT analysis, PEST analysis and Ansoff matrix will be used to analyse the findings from the above, as well as supplementary sources where needed.

▲ The introduction is good because it briefly provides background information about the business organization and it gives a clear outline of the issue under investigation.

▲ It is good practice to restate the research question at the end of the introduction, as it helps to focus the reader's mind (as well as yours, as you develop your commentary).

▲ This paragraph is useful with the list of supporting documents used and the list of the tools applied to reach the conclusion. They could also have been in bullet points. The reference to "supplementary sources where needed" indicates that the candidate did some further contextual research, beyond the supporting documents. This is not essential, but it can help better understand the organization, the topic, the issue.

---

[1] Interbrand. "Best Brands." Interbrand, 2016, www.interbrand.com/best-brands/best-global-brands/2016/ranking/burberry/

[2] Burberry. "BRAND, BUSINESS, CULTURE, TALENT." Careers at Burberry, burberrycareers.com/content/brand/

SWOT analysis

Strengths	Weaknesses
• Most followed luxury brand on social media (46 million followers on Instagram, Supporting Document 2)	• High prices limit available market
• Recognized as "Genius" ranking in digital innovation[3]	• High operating cost (Supporting Document 2)
• Strong celebrity endorsements. starting with George Mallory to modern day Kris Wu (Supporting Document 2)	• Limited product mix, consisting of only apparel, accessories and beauty products
• Brand recognition with check pattern print[4]	
• Strong brand name. ranked 18th luxury brand (Supporting Document 1)	
Opportunities	**Threats**
• Weaker pound due to Brexit attracting foreign tourist, especially Chinese[5]	• Parallel markets are rampant in high potential markets, like China[6]
• Many luxury market purchases made by travelers (Supporting Document 1)	• China's economy is slowing down[7]
• Market shift towards digitization and online shopping (Supporting Document 2)	• Increased availability of fake/imitation products[8]
• Rapid rise of middle class in China (Supporting Document 4)	

> ▲ The candidate shows how their supporting documents have helped them build their SWOT matrix (Criterion A).

> ▲ The SWOT matrix is well presented (Criterion G). The sources are always indicated, except for some cases of "general knowledge" that do not require a source.

> ▼ In a SWOT analysis, the opportunities and threats are external; they are identified in a PEST analysis…which the candidate conducted after the SWOT analysis. This is not logical; it shows that the candidate does not understand the relationship between these two models (Criterion B). PEST must always come before SWOT.

Figure 1: SWOT analysis for Burberry's in China

A SWOT analysis is a planning method that allows a business to evaluate the internal and external factors that may affect its success. From the figure above, Burberry has many strengths in comparison to its weaknesses, many related to how the company has built and maintained its brand. However, the threats to Burberry challenge their strengths, like imitation products lowering brand value. Despite this, the opportunities for Burberry complement their strengths well. The weaker pound due to Brexit should increase Burberry's sales in its home country, due to the influx of tourists, as almost half of the luxury's market purchases are by travellers. Furthermore, the digitalization of the world's markets also plays to Burberry's innovative strengths.

> ▲ The footnotes show the sources of further information, beyond the supporting documents.

[3] "L2 Digital lQ Index Rankings." L2: Benchmarking Digital Performance, 2017, www.l2inc.com/12-digital-iq-index-rankings
[4] Kent, Chuck, et al. "Burberry, the Icon of Fashion Brands." Brandingmag, Brandingmag Narrating the discussion, 17 July 2017, www.brandingmag.com/2011/08/10/burberry-icon-of-fashion-brands/
[5] Armstrong, Ashley. "Burberry revenues boosted by success in UK and China." The Telegraph, Telegraph Media Group, 12 July 2017, https://www.telegraph.co.uk/business/2017/07/12/burberry-revenues-boosted-success-uk-china/
[6] Schindler, Jacob. "China's move to curb grey market for luxury goods may have opposite effect." World Trademark Review, 16 Feb. 2017, www.worldtrademarkreview.com
[7] Iskyan, Kim. "Here's the real reason the global economy is slowing down." TheStreet, TheStreet, 12 July 2016, https://www.thestreet.com/story/13634929/1/here-s-the-real-reason-the-global-economy-is-slowing-down.html
[8] "Global trade in fake goods worth nearly half a trillion dollars a year - OECD & EUIPO." OECD, 18 Apr. 201 6, www.oecd.org/industry/global-trade-in-fake-goods worth-nearly-half-a-trillion-dol1ars-a-year.htm

PEST analysis

As Burberry is in a good position internally, the external factors that may affect Burberry were explored more, through a PEST analysis.

PEST analysis for Burberry's penetration of the Chinese market

Political

China has had issues with corruption, leading to anti-corruption regulations and government austerity measures, limiting the purchase of luxury items. This was a large reason why the potential market remained untapped. However, the anti-corruption movement has begun diminishing and consumer interest in luxury goods begun to rise.

However, a parallel market has risen, fuelled by personal shoppers, known as daigou, who bulk buy luxury goods overseas and import them into China to sell at cheaper prices.[9] This may cause decreased revenue for businesses, despite high operating costs. Furthermore, this dilutes the brand value, as imitation products are often sold as genuine, causing a misperception of quality. This is prevalent in one of China's largest online retailers, Tmall by Alibaba. As such, many luxury brands have left the retailer, however, this reduces a brand's market exposure, leaving businesses stuck in a dilemma[10].

To combat this, China has raised taxes on imported packages and cracked down on daigou[11]. While this has been somewhat successful in increasing domestic spending on luxury goods, it has also decreased China's overseas spending. This means that to access the potential of the Chinese market, it is necessary for companies like Burberry to expand more into China. Not doing so risks losing customers to the daigou, especially because of increased cost of purchasing from overseas, potentially damaging the Burberry brand[12].

Economic

China's economy is a global player, with a large population and GDP of $11,212 billion USD[13]. However, China's growth has slowed, falling from 10.3% in 2010 to 6.7% in 2016 (Supporting Document 4). Despite this, the economy is growing at a fast rate, with most consumers spending more or equal on luxury goods as the previous year (Supporting Document 1).

Another major economic factor is Brexit, as the weaker pound causes an influx of tourists, who will spend on companies like Burberry in the UK. However, it is also possible that operating costs will increase, as imported raw goods will be more expensive.

Nonetheless, the main effect of Brexit is that the U.K. will become an independent economy. As part of the EU, the UK is also part of

[9] Schindler, Jacob. "China's move to curb grey market for luxury goods may have opposite effect." World Trademark Review, 16 Feb. 2017, www.worldtrademarkreview.com
[10] Flora, Liz. "Coach's Tmall Shop Closes as Luxury Brands Turn To WeChat Sales." King Daily, 23 Sept. 2016, jingdaily.com/coachs-tma11-shop-closes-as-luxury-brands-turn to-wechat-sales/
[11] "China's Grey Luxury Market Threatened by New Tax Regime." Fortune, 3 Apr. 2016. fortune.com/2016/04/03/chinas-grey-1uxury-market-taxes/
[12] Schindler, Jacob. "China's move to curb grey market for luxury goods may have opposite effect." World Trademark Review, 16 Feb. 2017, www.worldtrademarkreview.com
[13] "China's Economic Outlook in Six Charts." IMF, 15 Aug. 2017, www.imforg/en/Ncws/Articles/2017/08/09/NA081517-China-Economic-Outlook-in-Six-Charts

the EU's single market as mentioned earlier. This means all member countries can free trade with each other, allowing an uninhibited movement of products and people across borders. While this can improve productivity and lower prices, this also takes away control from each country. Furthermore, all EU countries must charge the same import duties to non-EU members (Supporting Document 5). This has been a hindrance in striking trade deals with countries like China. However, leaving the single market due to Brexit means the U.K. can negotiate better deals with other countries. This allows companies like Burberry to operate in China with less restrictions and lower costs, allowing them to pass this lowered cost down to customers.

Social

China boasts a population of over 1.3 billion people, with more than 75% of the population to be middle-class by the year 2030[14]. In times past, Chinese spending has been centered around necessities, however, as the society wealthier, consumer habits are changing. The older generation of Chinese people who have survived through tough economic situations, chose to save rather than spend, resulting in the average Chinese citizen having 26% more savings than the global average[15]. However, this is changing, with working-age consumers (ages 18–56), are spending more on premium products over cheaper, mass-market products (Supporting Document 4). This social change and demand for premium products is the perfect opportunity for luxury brands like Burberry and its products.

▲ The PEST analysis is well applied to the topic of Burberry in China (Criterion B).

Technological

In China's emerging market, digital technology plays a big role. China's online community consists of more than 700 million smartphone and Internet users, led by the mushrooming middle class. Purchases made on WeChat, a chatting application, have doubled between 2015 and 2016, with 60% purchasing apparel in-app (Supporting Document 4). This is a significant opportunity for Burberry, as it is unique in its digital innovation for a luxury brand.

▲ Such statements show the candidate's ability to evaluate (Criterion E).

Through the PEST analysis of external factors, Burberry is in an advantageous position to further penetrate the Chinese market. Exploiting the social change early will allow Burberry to build a customer base before other brands. Furthermore, while the other factors may also apply to other luxury brands, the technological external factor that only Burberry will be able to exploit to its fullest.

Ansoff matrix

An Ansoff matrix shows how a company's strategy may differ based on whether they are selling a new or existing product in a new or existing market.

▼ This is correct but the candidate should have written more about market penetration in order to achieve an even higher mark for Criterion B. The application of the Ansoff matrix is correct, but it should be more developed, with at least one or two sentences.

As Burberry are trying to increase consumers in an existing market with an existing product, they fit under market penetration. Burberry achieves this through the development and innovation of their digital technologies. This is exemplified through Burberry's digital marketing strategy using WeChat. WeChat is a mobile app in China, with more than 600 million users, with around 60% using WeChat for information

[14] Chandran, Nyshka. "China will be middle class by 2030, with high earners to rise 1,000% in some cities." CNBC, CNBC, 3 Nov. 2016, www.cnbc.com/2016/11/02/china-will-be-middle-income-by-2030with-spending-on-cars-luxuries-health-to-rise.html

[15] "China's Economic Outlook in Six Charts." IMF, 15 Aug. 2017, https://www.imf.org/en/News/Articles/2017/08/09/NA081517-China-Economic-Outlook-in-Six-Charts

on luxury products (Supporting Document 3). Burberry has used this app to disseminate information to customers and promote traffic to their official site. This increases awareness of the brand among the key target audience, the middle-class Chinese. Furthermore, Burberry operates customer service through the app, usually responding within 24 hours. This emphasizes its dedication to the best service; appealing to Chinese customers who are seeking the best.

> ▲ This good analysis will enable the candidate to achieve a higher mark for Criteria C and E.

Burberry also increases brand awareness through celebrity endorsements. One example is with Kris Wu, a Chinese-born singer, actor, and model. He is also a former lead member of the famous boy group Exo, meaning that lie is a household name in China (Supporting Document 2). Such endorsements build brand equity for Burberry in a market where they are not as well known. Furthermore, it will differentiate Burberry from other Western competitors, as a Chinese-born ambassador is more likely to attract a Chinese audience than a Caucasian model.

> ▲ Another instance that shows the candidate's evaluative skills (Criterion E).

Conclusion

Overall, Burberry should penetrate the Chinese market further, regardless of Brexit.

> ▼ This sentence seems to answer the following question:
>
> "Should Burberry penetrate the Chinese market further?"
>
> The research question, stated in the introduction, is however slightly different:
>
> "To what extent will Brexit affect Burberry's penetration of the Chinese market?"
>
> As a consequence, the candidate will not be able to achieve maximum marks for Criterion D.

However, Brexit provides an excellent economic opportunity to start and precede other luxury firms. While there may be short-term problems, like acquiring a customer base and competing against parallel markets, the long term benefits the emergent middle-class Chinese can bring outweigh these negatives. A solution to these short-term problems can be to strengthen products in the U.K. for the tourists traveling due to the weak pound caused by Brexit. In China, Burberry should continue innovating and marketing digitally, as it has been successful. By establishing a strong foothold in the Chinese market now, aided by Brexit, Burberry can exploit the huge luxury market in the future when other competitors struggle to penetrate the market.

<u>Works cited</u>

<u>Supporting documents:</u>

1. Arienti, Patrizia. "Global Powers of Luxury Goods 2017"

2. Deloitte., 2017. Burberry. "Annual Report 2016/17", 2017, Web

3. Milnes, Hilary. "How Burberry became the top digital luxury brand." Digiday, 20 Mar. 2017, digiday.com/marketing/burberry-became-top-digital-luxury-brand/

4. "The CEO guide to China's future." McKinsey & Company, Sept. 2016, www.mckinsey.com/featured-insights/china/the-ceo-guide-to-chinas-future

5. Wheeler, Alex Hunt & Brian. "Brexit: All you need to know about the UK leaving the EU." BBC News, BBC, 9 Oct. 2017, www.bbc.co.uk/news/uk-politics-32810887

> ▲ The candidate clearly indicates the sources of the five supporting documents they have used to build their case.

<u>Others:</u>

Armstrong, Ashley. "Burberry revenues boosted by success in UK and China." The Telegraph, Telegraph Media Group, 12 July 2017, www.telegraph.co.uk/business/2017/07/12/burberry-revenues-boosted-success-uk-china/

Interbrand. "Best Brands." Interbrand, 2016, www.interbrand.com/best-brands/best-global-brands/2016/ranking/burberry/

Burberry. "BRAND, BUSINESS, CULTURE, TALENT." Careers at Burberry, burberrycareers.com/content/brand/

> ▲ The candidate did some further research to have more information and more data about the context. This is not compulsory, though most candidates do it. Extra research does not attract extra marks.

Chandran, Nyshka. "China will be middle class by 2030, with high earners to rise 1,000% in some cities." CNBC, CNBC, 3 Nov. 2016, www.cnbc.com/2016/11/02/china-will-be-middle-income-by-2030with-spending-on-cars-luxuries-health-to-rise.html

"China's Economic Outlook in Six Charts." IMF, 15 Aug. 2017, www.imforg/en/Ncws/Articles/2017/08/09/NA081517-China-Economic-Out1ook-in-Six-Charts

"China's Grey Luxury Market Threatened by New Tax Regime." Fortune, 3 Apr. 2016. fortune.com/2016/04/03/chinas-grey-1uxury-market-taxes/

Flora, Liz. "Coach's Tmall Shop Closes as Luxury Brands Turn To WeChat Sales." King Daily, 23 Sept. 2016, jingdaily.com/coachs-tma11-shop-closes-as-luxury-brands-turn to-wechat-sales/

"Global trade in fake goods worth nearly half a trillion dollars a year - OECD & EUIPO." OECD, 18 Apr. 2016, www.oecd.org/industry/global-trade-in-fake-goods worth-nearly-half-a-trillion-dol1ars-a-year.htm

Iskyan, Kim. "Here's the real reason the global economy is slowing down." TheStreet, TheStreet, 12 July 2016, https://www.thestreet.com/story/13634929/1/here-s-the-real-reason-the-global-economy-is-slowing-down.html

Kent, Chuck, et al. "Burberry, the Icon of Fashion Brands." Brandingmag, Brandingmag Narrating the discussion, 17 July 2017, www.brandingmag.com/2011/08/10/burberry-icon-of-fashion-brands/

"L2 Digital lQ Index Rankings." L2: Benchmarking Digital Performance, 2017, www.l2inc.com/12-digital-iq-index-rankings

Schindler, Jacob. "China's move to curb grey market for luxury goods may have opposite effect." World Trademark Review, 16 Feb. 2017, www.worldtrademarkreview.com

The callout reads: ▲ All these sources are mentioned in the document, and vice versa.

What marks were awarded for this written commentary?

This very good commentary scored 22 out of 25:

Criterion	Mark	Out of	Justification
A	4	4	The five documents are relevant and sufficiently in-depth. They come from a range of sources (internal, external) and offer several perspectives, as required to achieve 4 marks for Criterion A. The external sources are reliable, such as the BBC or McKinsey & Company.
B	4	5	SWOT, PEST and Ansoff are well used in this IA, although having SWOT *before* PEST shows that the candidate does not understand how PEST is an external analysis that helps formulate the O and T of SWOT. The Ansoff matrix is correctly applied, but the candidate could have further developed their analysis in terms of market penetration. For these reasons, a mark of 4 rather than 5 is awarded for B.
C	4	5	There is an appropriate selection of data from the supporting documents (and other sources, when necessary, as indicated by the candidate at the end of the introduction) with good analysis and integration of ideas. For an even higher mark, the analysis could have been even more skilful, for example considering that China is only one of Burberry's many markets.
D	2	3	The conclusion only partly answers the research question, which was "To what extent will Brexit affect Burberry's penetration of the Chinese market?". The conclusion seems to answer the following question: "Should Burberry further penetrate the Chinese market?". The two are not different; in this case, the research question should probably have been revised. In order to achieve 3 marks for Criterion D, the conclusion must answer the research question as formulated.

Continued on next page

Criterion	Mark	Out of	Justification
E	4	4	There is evidence of evaluation throughout the IA, and the judgments are well substantiated.
F	2	2	The structure is appropriate (the candidate is not penalized again under Criterion F for the order of SWOT and PEST).
G	2	2	This commentary is well presented. All the elements are present (cover page, table of contents, page numbers etc.). The layout is clear.
Total:	22	25	With a score of 22, this very good commentary scores a grade 7. Only minor aspects could have been even better, for example a tighter fit between the research question and the conclusion.

Internal assessment at higher level

Your task

Your IA task at HL is a research project. This project involves two key elements. The first element is to prepare a research proposal (500 words maximum) outlining your plan to help a real organization make a business decision or to address an issue facing that organization. The second element is to collect and analyse data to formulate recommendations about that decision or to address the issue identified (2000 words maximum). This assignment gives you the opportunity to carry out primary research (for example interviewing the business owner) and to apply, to a real business decision or issue, the skills and knowledge gained from the business management course.

Examples of recent titles

Should PetroKazakhstan recruit a new in-house translator or outsource this service, in order to solve the regional director's increasing workload?	This is a **good** research question which identifies the two options that will be compared and contrasted in the IA. The question also outlines why there is a need for this research ("to solve the director's increasing workload"), which is why the company may benefit from the findings and recommendation.
Should Malaysia Airports Holdings Berhad (MAHB) invest in building a factory outlet centre to increase its commercial revenue?	This is a **good** research question because it will be possible to answer the question ("yes" or "no") after investment analysis and appraisal. The question also identifies the aim ("to increase commercial revenue") and thus the rationale for the research.
To what extent and how are McDonald's employees motivated?	This is **not** a good research question for several reasons. It is too vague (McDonald's employees where? In a specific country, in a specific restaurant?), the wording is unclear ("to what extent and how") and there is no clear business decision at the heart of the enquiry. This title is also likely to result in a descriptive project that will earn few marks for analysis and evaluation (Criterion D) and also for recommendations (Criterion F). A better title could be "How can the manager of Maryville McDonald's increase employees' motivation and thereby lower their absenteeism and the high turnover?"
Why did Carlos Martinez Ltd. invest in a new truck?	This is **not** a good research question because it is backward-looking. Although the question suggests what the IA will cover (interview with the business owner, investment appraisal), the decision to invest in a new vehicle has already been made. A better question could be "Should Carlos Martinez hire a new part-time truck driver or redeploy his existing workforce?"

The assessment criteria

Your teacher will mark your IA using nine criteria, A to I:

- Criterion **A** assesses your research proposal (and only this first document).

- Criterion **B** assesses your primary sources and primary data.

- Criterion **C** assesses your use of tools, theories and techniques from the curriculum.

- Criterion **D** assesses your ability to analyse and evaluate your findings.

- Criterion **E** assesses the conclusions you reach at the end of your research.

- Criterion **F** assesses the recommendations you formulate for your chosen organization.

- Criterion **G** assesses the structure of your work.

- Criterion **H** assesses the presentation of your work.

- Criterion **I** assesses your ability to reflect critically on your approach taken and its limitations.

Criterion A: Research proposal (up to 3 marks)

To achieve a high mark for Criterion A, you must include all the following elements, in this precise order:

- Your research question.

- The rationale for your study, i.e. why the research is important for the business. It must be a commercial rationale, not a personal one: many students lose marks, because they do not justify the value for the business, for example they write "I chose this topic because I want to take a degree in marketing" or "because this is my family business". This may be a reason for choosing the business or the topic, but it is not a business rationale.

- Your proposed methodology, including:

  o the areas of the syllabus you will cover (it is enough to state the sub-units names/numbers)

  o the main sources of information you will use

  o the organizations and individuals you will approach

  o the methods you will use to collect and analyse data, and your reason(s) for choosing them.

- The difficulties you anticipate, such as limited responses or biased sources (you could also comment on potential solutions for the anticipated difficulties, although these are not directly assessed by Criterion A).

- Your action plan: the order of activities and timescale of the project (you can use a Gantt chart for this).

Many students do no score top marks because they forget to include one of these elements. As the word limit for the proposal is tight (500 words), it is important that you remain concise; use bullet points: this is how business documents are presented.

Criterion B: Sources and data (up to 3 marks)

To achieve a high mark for Criterion B, your primary sources and primary data must be appropriate, varied and sufficient. Two sources may be enough, but three or more offer more evidence and more perspectives. It is important that you go beyond the partial views of the owners or managers of the business; this may mean asking customers, suppliers or other stakeholders for their views. As the focus of the task is primary research, you will need to interact with people; collecting documents from the company or from their website is not enough. Most students do interviews and use questionnaires/surveys, but other methods are possible too, such as conducting a focus group.

Criterion C: Use of tools, techniques and theories (up to 3 marks)

To achieve a high mark for Criterion C, your tools, techniques and theories must be (i) relevant and (ii) well applied. Many students over-rely on poorly written SWOT analyses and PEST analyses; SWOT and PEST are not always suitable. They may help you understand the organization and its context, but few IA research questions can be answered with a SWOT or PEST analysis alone. There are many other tools, such as position maps, product life cycles, Ansoff matrix, fishbone analysis, break-even, decision trees and sales forecasting that students rarely use, and that could nonetheless be employed to support the investigation of the research question. As you work on your research project, check the contents of the syllabus to see which tools you could use – and think beyond PEST and SWOT.

Criterion D: Analysis and evaluation (up to 6 marks)

To achieve a high mark for Criterion D, you must do the following:

- Analyse the data that you have collected, by applying your chosen tools; this way, you will gradually interpret your results and findings.

- Evaluate your judgments, making an appraisal based on the evidence that you have collected and analysed, for example comparing two options or two courses of action.

- Integrate your ideas, which means that you must not consider each source separately ("The first interview shows that…", "The second interview shows that…") but you must link your arguments together in a coherent way (for example "Arguments for…", "Arguments against…").

Criterion E: Conclusions (up to 2 marks)

To achieve a high mark for Criterion E, you must ensure that your conclusions are consistent with the evidence presented in the main body of the report and that you do not add any new information, new data or new analysis. Your conclusion must relate to your research question and be based on your research findings. A good conclusion can be relatively short, as long as it addresses the assessment criteria.

Criterion F: Recommendations (up to 2 marks)

To achieve a high mark for Criterion F, your recommendations must be substantiated, and in line with your findings and your conclusions. The conclusions are more academic, whereas the recommendations are written for the organization itself. Your recommendations may be relatively short, as long as they answer the research question. Bullet pointing key recommendations is acceptable. Areas for further study must be identified to achieve 2 marks.

Criterion G: Structure (up to 2 marks)

To achieve a high mark for Criterion G, the structure of your IA should be logical and flow well with an argument that is easy to follow. The most common reason why candidates do not reach 2 marks is the fact that they separately apply different analytical tools, which makes it very hard for the marker and moderator to understand the coherence of the IA.

Criterion H: Presentation (up to 2 marks)

To achieve a high mark for Criterion H the presentation of your IA should follow exactly the written report layout from the *Business management guide* on pages 81 and 82. The vast majority of students do not get awarded 2 marks for Criterion H because they modify the model or forget one of the sections. The structure of the IA at higher level is very prescriptive, unlike the structure of the IA at standard level. A key difficulty is the fact that you have two separate documents (the research proposal and the written report) but they are merged into one for their final submission; this can be a source of confusion, as it means, for example, that your table of contents is not at the start of the file, but at the start of the second document.

Criterion I: Reflective thinking (up to 2 marks)

To achieve a high mark for Criterion I, you must reflect critically on your research approach and the limitations of your work. You can do this in any part of your report, for example in the section where you summarize your findings, or in the conclusions. Some students prefer to create a sub-section for these reflections. It is not a reflection on the organization, on its activities and issues it faces; it is a reflection on your own research, for example about the validity and reliability of your findings, the size and representativeness of the sample of customers you spoke to, or the lack of objectivity of some people you interviewed.

Grade boundaries

The grade boundaries at higher level are the following ones:

Grade	1	2	3	4	5	6	7
Mark range	0–3	4–6	7–9	10–12	13–14	15–17	18–25

This shows you that to achieve a grade 7, you do not need to get top marks for all the criteria, as you only need to get 18 marks overall.

Five tips for your IA

1	You may focus your IA on *any part of the syllabus*, however including *quantitative* elements (e.g. about an investment decision) works well for the IA at higher level. With projects on marketing or HR, there is a risk of remaining superficial or over-generalizing. Of course, you can still do very well and score very highly with a topic on HR and marketing, but it can be more difficult, especially if there is a need to quantify your recommendations. All business decisions usually have financial implications, as there are cost implications to all recommended courses of action.
2	In general, a *small local* organization is often a very good choice. If your teacher allows it, you may choose your family business, but you should then consider issues of objectivity/subjectivity, as well as the appropriateness of the primary research you may want to carry out. It is not appropriate to interview the employees and ask them what they think about your parents' leadership style – and you cannot simply chat with your parents about their business and call this "research".
3	The scenario of this research project is that you are a *consultant* working for the organization, employed by the managers to help them solve a problem and come up with a solution to make a decision. This is why you must write *recommendations* at the end of your research project, answering directly the research question and written for the business, telling them what they should do, based on your research. This is fundamentally different from the EE where you are a scholar.

4	Your analysis may be deeper and more convincing if you include some elements from the "**HL only**" part of the curriculum (e.g. planning tools such as force field analysis or decision tree, see 1.7, or financial tools such as efficiency ratio, see 3.6). This is not a requirement of the IA though: you could do very well using only SL/HL core content; what matters is that you use relevant tools, theories and techniques (Criterion C).
5	It is recommended that you spend **30 hours** on your research project. Many candidates spend even more, especially to organize the primary research, collect data and then analyse it. It is therefore important that you choose the organization very carefully, defining the research question with them. You do not need to have access to confidential data from the company, so it is not a problem if they are reluctant to share financial data with you, such as their financial accounts: depending on your research question, it is not necessary – but what is necessary is the primary research.

Structure

As the structure is very prescriptive (see Criterion H) you may want to use the template that follows. It is precisely based on the IB format and requirements.

Business management
Higher level
Internal assessment

Examination session:

May 2020 ●━━━━━━━━━━━━━━━━━━ Change accordingly.

Research question:

Write your research question here, ending with a question mark.

Word count:

Research proposal: *xxx* words   *(max 500 words)*

Executive summary: *xxx* words   *(max 200 words)*

Written report: *xxx* words   *(max 2000 words)*

Research proposal

Research question

Write your research question here (again).

Rationale for study

Write one paragraph, around 80 words.

Proposed methodology

- Areas of syllabus to be covered

These are just examples – replace with yours. Recommendation: use the unit numbers.

Syllabus unit	Area to be covered	Reason
5.3 Lean production	Benchmarking	Comparison with competitors and industry standards

- Possible sources of information

This is just an example – replace with yours.

This is just an example – replace with yours. You must have primary: interviews, questionnaires etc.

Type of source	Source	Reason
Secondary	Reports from the Chamber of Commerce	Collect data about local industry trends
Primary	Interview with the manager	Get his/her internal perspective

- Organizations and individuals to be approached

Mr CM, manager…

- Methods for data collection and analysis

Examples, to be replaced by yours.

Technique	Reason
SWOT analysis	To understand the current position of the business, both internally and externally
Fishbone diagram	To map and analyse the possible reasons for the decrease in customer number and the increase of negative reputation

Anticipated difficulties

Examples, to be replaced by yours.

- Not enough people may answer my survey.
- I am related to the manager and I know his restaurant very well, which may be a source of bias.

Action plan

The order of activities and timescale of the project

You could use a Gantt chart indicating timing, days, weeks.

Remember: 500 words maximum, so your research proposal must be concise.

Written Report

Content of the research project

This research project is written by *your name* to help Business *YYY* decide if…

> Add yours.

It answers the following research question:
(COPY YOUR RESEARCH QUESTION AGAIN)

> You may have the impression that this repeats the line just before it a little.

The intended audience is twofold: the manager of *YYY* and the teacher/supervisor.

> Add yours.

Word count of the research project:

1862 Words (plus 172 words Abstract)

> Replace with your own word counts.

Acknowledgements

I would like to thank *XXXXX* and *YYYYY*…

> Add yours.

Contents page:

> Add your own page numbers. Note: this does not start at "1" because of the research proposal.

Executive summary:

The purpose of this project was to answer the following research question: "…"

The starting point was…The scope of the investigation was…

Methodologically,…

This project concluded that…

The project recommended that…

> 200 words maximum – it is NOT in the total word count of 2000 words for the main "research report".
>
> You do not have to use these specific terms, as long as your executive summary (abstract) includes the following three key elements:
>
> - The research question.
> - The scope of the investigation and methodology employed.
> - The conclusions and recommendations reached.
>
> Of course, you can only write the abstract at the end, once you have finished your project and you know what your conclusion and recommendations are!

Introduction

Present the business, the research question and the rationale – like at the start of your proposal – suggestion: around 200 words.

Research question

Copy it. (Again!)

Methodology employed

Type of source	Source	Reason
Secondary	Reports from the Chamber of Commerce	Collect data about local industry trends
Primary	Interview with the manager	Get his/her internal perspective

Technique	Reason for its use
Fishbone diagram	To map and analyse the possible reasons for the decrease in customer number and the increase of negative reputation (word of mouth)

> This will repeat your proposal, though there might be some differences between what you initially planned to do (in your proposal) and what you actually did (in your research itself).

Main results and findings

In this section, outline what you have found. There is no analysis yet, and no use of business tools, theories and techniques. You can briefly summarize what you were told in the interviews, you may include the results of your surveys, for example with pie charts. Suggestion: 1 page, 2 pages....but not too much! (All the raw data will be in your appendices: the transcript of the interviews, the results from your survey etc.).

Analysis and discussion

This is the most important section, over several pages. This is where you use the tools, theories and techniques (e.g. fishbone, force field analysis, ratio calculations…) and where you create arguments and ideas. You interpret the data you have collected, you give sense to it…This is a long section, it is "the core" of your IA. Make sure the "internal structure" of the section is coherent and logical: this is essential for Criterion G.

Conclusions and recommendations

Conclusions

Summarize what you have found and analysed, but do not add new data or new ideas.

Recommendations

Make the recommendations very clear e.g. "purchase…", "invest in…", "choose…" Mention (1) the limitations of your research (e.g. your awareness that your results are limited because…), (2) areas for further research (i.e. if you could, what else you would research on this, to have a more complete answer).

xx

References and bibliography

Books

Websites

xxxxxxxxxxxxxxxxxxxxxxxxxxxxxxxxxxxxxxxxxxxxxxxxxxxxxxxxxxxxxx

Appendix 1

Interview of *XXX* **(date).**

Add, if you have conducted an interview.

Transcript of the interview.

Appendix 2

Add, if you have used a questionnaire.

Blank copy of the questionnaire.

Add other appendices, depending on your research project – maybe PEST analysis and SWOT analysis, as part of your background preparation. Remember though that anything placed in the appendices, including any additional tools or business techniques, cannot be rewarded under the assessment criteria.

PRACTICE EXAM PAPER 2

At this point, you will have re-familiarized yourself with the content from the topics of the IB business management syllabus. Additionally, you will have picked up some key techniques and skills to refine your exam approach. It is now time to put these skills to the test; in this section you will find a practice examination paper 2, with the same structure as the external assessment you will complete at the end of the DP course.

Section A

Answer **one** question from this section.

1. La Vaquita (LV)

In the Mexican state of Querétaro, a group of five dairy farmers have decided to set up a cooperative named *La Vaquita* (*LV*). Working together will enable them to achieve economies of scale. The cooperative's initial capital is $8000.

The farmers have forecasted the following figures for the first six months of operation, beginning in July:

Sales

- Average selling price of each piece of cheese: $4.
- 3000 pieces of cheese will be sold in July, and 4000 pieces per month from August onwards.
- One half of the production will be sold directly to customers, who will pay cash, in the cooperative store. The other half will be sold to supermarkets, on credit, payable one month later.

Costs

- Rent: $4500 per month.
- Labour costs: $2500 per month.
- Raw materials: 40% of sales revenue every month, paid in cash.
- Overheads: $1100 per month, paid in cash.

  a) Describe **one** advantage of *LV* being a cooperative. [2]

  b) Explain how *LV* will help the dairy farmers achieve economies of scale. [2]

  c) Prepare a monthly cash flow forecast for *LV* for the first six months of operation (July to December). [6]

2. Abhinav Awasthi's construction business

Abhinav Awasthi has a small construction business in Pune, India. He has worked as a sole trader for the last 10 years, since he opened is business. However, he is now thinking about changing legal status and registering as a private limited company.

With the help of his accountant, Abhinav has started to prepare the following figures for his final accounts.

Selected financial information, as at 31 May (all figures in $)

Cash	55 000
Cost of goods sold	3 000 000
Creditors	45 000
Debtors	X
Expenses	2 300 000
Fixed assets	350 000
Loan capital	40 000
Retained profit	215 000
Sales revenue	5 600 000
Share capital	200 000
Short-term loan	10 000
Stock	50 000

a) Define the term *fixed assets*. [2]

b) Explain **one** advantage for Abhinav of registering his business as a private limited company. [2]

c) Using relevant information from the table, construct a balance sheet and calculate debtors (figure X). [6]

Section B

Answer **one** question from this section.

3. Barberia Checho

Barberia Checho is a barbershop located in Medellín, Colombia. Sergio Valdez, the owner, works as a sole trader. Besides Sergio himself, there are four other barbers: Cesar, Fredy, Jairo and Jorge. However, they are not Sergio's employees in a traditional sense: he does not pay them, but rather they rent a space in his barbershop with a chair, mirror and dressing table. Each barber receives 50% of the price paid by the customers whose hair he cuts; the other 50% goes to Sergio. This is the usual business model for barbershops in Colombia and in some other countries.

Although there are many barbershops in the neighbourhood, *Barberia Checho* is very popular and very busy. Its normal opening hours are 11am to 9pm, but it often stays open later, until 10pm or 11pm, if there are more customers waiting to have their hair cut.

Cesar and Fredy know that the success of *Barberia Checho* is largely due to their own reputation as excellent barbers, and they ask for more money. Sergio hesitates. If he refuses, he fears that Cesar and Fredy may decide to leave and go to work for one of his competitors, but he has many direct costs and indirect costs, and the current model suits him.

a) State **one** direct cost and **one** indirect cost that *Barberia Checho* may have. [2]

b) Explain **two** advantages for Sergio of operating as a sole trader. [4]

c) Suggest **two** pricing strategies that may be appropriate for *Barberia Checho*. [4]

d) Examine whether Sergio should change the system of financial rewards he uses with his barbers. [10]

4. Accor

Accor is a French hotel company that operates in 100 countries. It has 4200 hotels that employ 250 000 people. Some hotels are directly owned by *Accor*, others operate through a franchise.

Accor has 26 brands that target different market segments, offering a range of prices (from $50 a night to over $1000 a night) and a range of styles (from classic and traditional, to modern, entertaining and more youthful):

- Some premium brands (luxury, upscale), such as *Sofitel* and *Pullman*, offer more classic hotels, typically targeting business people.

- The premium brand *Mama Shelter*, which was recently launched, offers a more modern and entertaining look.

- With almost 500 hotels throughout the world, the classic brand *Novotel* is midscale (neither luxury, nor budget).

- *Accor* also has some low-cost (budget, economy) brands, such as *Ibis Budget* (more classic) and *Jo&Joe* (more modern and entertaining).

Accor has a loyalty membership scheme called "Le Club AccorHotels": guests earn points and benefits according to the number of nights they spend in hotels that belong to *Accor*.

Accor's corporate social responsibility (CSR) is often praised as a model of good practice in the hospitality industry. In 2015, the consultancy group *Accenture* carried out a large-scale study in over 1200 *Accor* hotels and found the following:

- CSR has a positive effect on guests' satisfaction.

- CSR has a positive effect on hotel profitability.

a) Define the term *franchise*. [2]

b) Construct a positioning map (perception map) of *Accor* hotels. [4]

c) Explain the importance of *Accor's* CSR strategy to **one** internal stakeholder and to **one** external stakeholder. [4]

d) Discuss the importance of branding for *Accor*. [10]

5. Anti-Slavery International (ASI)

Anti-Slavery International (ASI) is an international NGO (non-governmental organization) based in London, UK. It fights against slavery and human trafficking worldwide. It is the world's oldest international human rights organization.

ASI revenue:

ASI has several revenue streams. One third of its revenue is from donations from individuals, community groups and companies. Two thirds come from British and international government grants, trusts, foundations and institutional funders.

ASI expenditure:

ASI directly spends almost 90% of its revenue on anti-slavery projects in countries such as Nepal, Tanzania, Turkmenistan and Vietnam. The rest is spent on fundraising, campaigning and social marketing. As a charity, *ASI* reinvests any surplus.

ASI, like most charities, works with volunteers, both in its London office and in the countries where its projects take place. By definition, volunteers are not paid, although they may usually claim for some money, for example as reimbursement for their lunch or their travel expenses. Volunteers are not motivated by financial rewards, but by other intrinsic factors, such as the opportunity to make a difference, teamwork or the experience itself.

a) Define the term *revenue stream*. [2]

b) Explain the sentence: "As a charity, *ASI* reinvests any surplus". [3]

c) With reference to *ASI*, explain the differences between commercial marketing and social marketing. [5]

d) To what extent can motivation theories be applied to volunteers? [10]

Section C

Answer **one** question from this section. The organizations featured in sections A and B and in the paper 1 case study may not be used as a basis to your answer.

6. With reference to an organization of your choice, discuss the impact of **globalization** on its marketing **strategy**. [20]

7. With reference to an organization of your choice, examine the impact of **culture** and **ethics** on the organization. [20]

8. With reference to an organization of your choice, discuss how internal and external factors cause some parts of the **strategy** to **change** over time. [20]